I0391039

Global Credit Crunch

Understanding the Fragility of Capitalism

Adnan Khan

مكتبة اسلامية Maktaba Islamia

MaktabaIslamia Publications

www.maktabaislamia.com
info@maktabaislamia.com
www.facebook.com/everythingislamic
www.twitter.com/maktabaislamia

2016 CE – 1437 H

Translation of the Qur'ān

It should be perfectly clear that the Qur'ān is only authentic in its original language, Arabic. Since perfect translation of the Qur'ān is impossible, we have used the translation of the meaning of the Qur'ān throughout the book, as the result is only a crude meaning of the Arabic text.

Qur'ānic verses appear in speech marks proceeded by a reference to the Surah and verse number. Sayings (*Hadith*) of Prophet Muhammad ﷺ appear in inverted commas along with reference to the Hadith Book and its Reporter.

صلى الله عليه وسلم - ﷺ (Peace be upon him)

سبحانه وتعالى - ﷻ (Glory to Him, the Exalted)

Contents

Introduction

Capitalism (economic Liberalism) has been credited for generating wealth that has been unprecedented in history. For many historians the struggle between Capitalism and Communism for global supremacy was settled through the ability of Capitalism to generate vast amounts of wealth and prosperity for its people. The battle between the two ideologies resulted in free markets, free trade, financial markets and the removal of state intervention in the economy becoming prerequisites for 21st century economies. Proponents of Capitalism continue to hold the development of South East Asia especially Japan as well as Germany were a direct result of the adoption of Capitalism.

The Third world has also not been spared, Indonesia, Pakistan, South America, Africa as well as the Middle East were all sold the idea of free markets, and all of these regions and nations now have Western style financial markets where large sums of wealth are the subject of speculation on the state of the economy and future revenue flows.

Malaysia was the first of the Muslim world to set up Western style financial markets which attracted many Western companies, hedge funds and even George Soro's (world renowned speculator). Pakistan's KSE 100 Index was the best-performing stock market index in the world as declared by the international magazine "Business Week" in 2004[1] It is currently valued more then $30 billion. The remainder of the Muslim world also have financial markets, with the Gulf States having the largest. However only those aligned to the rulers or from their families have benefited from the financial markets.

Although the Western world led by the US continue to sell Capitalism and its adoption as the only way for progress Capitalism has come to be characterised with the regular boom and bust, recession and even economic collapse. The 1997 Asian financial crisis has been attributed to liberal style financial markets, speculation and many nations such as Indonesia and Thailand a decade later have been unable to recover from the crisis.

The world is once again in the midst of a global crisis which began with the financial crisis, that engulfed the world. The 'Credit crunch' as it has come to be known brought panic and turmoil in the summer of 2007 to the world's financial markets causing the US housing market bubble to burst. The crisis threatens a worldwide economic recession, potentially bringing to a halt more than a decade of increasing prosperity and employment for Western economies and potentially wiping a staggering $1 trillion off of the value of the world economy.[2]

Many experts have commented on individual factors that caused the crisis, once again steering well clear of blaming Capitalism. As each month commenced from the summer of 2007 more and more information become clear about the extent of the problem. The collapse of Northern Rock, the 5th largest bank in the UK, the bankruptcies of nearly all of the Sub-prime providers in the US, the continued coordinated actions by the world's central banks in pumping billions into the financial markets and the stunning meltdown of Bear sterns, the 5th largest investment bank in the US in March 2008.

Whilst many individuals in the West were reeling from the credit crunch and contemplating queuing outside their bank to withdrew their savings in case their bank was next to collapse disturbing headlines made the front pages of all major newspapers in the West about the soaring cost of basic food commodities. The World Bank warned that these price levels will be maintained until the year 2015.[3] Many poor people around the world who already spend most of their disposable incomes on food are suddenly finding it impossible just to feed themselves. With riots and protests seen as far wide from Haiti to Indonesia, the lack of food has the potential to create geo-political upheaval.

With the global economy facing the very real possibility of recession and inflation – especially food inflation skyrocketing, the worlds most important and most traded resource reached unprecedented levels. In January 2008 the price of Oil passed the $100 mark when a single trader in search of market fame pushed through a small trade. By May 2008 the price of oil reached an unprecedented $135 a barrel. Oil has risen by 25% since January 2008 and by nearly 400% since the beginning of the 21st century. With Oil playing a key role in the functioning of Western economies they face an unprecedented crisis with key sectors on the verge of disaster.

The sudden rise in global commodity prices occurred in almost the same period as the global credit crunch crisis. Western bankers, economists and politicians have all failed to publicly link the crisis's and have dogmatically blamed China and India for consuming too much, greedy speculators, regulation and transparency.

The Global credit crunch, food crisis and oil crisis has once again highlighted the fragility of Capitalism, as the fallout from the credit crunch and the wider economic crisis continues, demands for alternatives are certain to grow. The aim of this book is to scutanise the causes of the current crisis and evaluate some concepts which go to the heart of Capitalism which will always cause such crisis. It will asses the various factors that have all contributed to the crisis and scrutanise why Capitalism regularly has economic crisis. The Islamic view on such factors will be presented in the form of an Islamic economy under the Khilafah in order to show how Islam will bring the much needed stability the world needs.

Adnan Khan
5th June 2008

Global Credit Crunch

The 'credit crunch' crisis that reverberated round the world was essentially an American created problem. Since gaining independence from Britain in 1776 the United States of America after 230 years has grown into a fully integrated, industrialised economy that manufacturer's 28% of the world's output. Barring a 'great depression' type catastrophe the US economy should be worth a mammoth $14 trillion by the end of the US tax year on October 2008. The 300 million people of the US generate more wealth then the next five nations combined and the US has been the world's largest economy every year since 1872.

Global Gross domestic product (GDP) 2007

1 US	13.8t
2 Japan	4.3t
3 Germany	3.3t
4 China	3.2t
5 UK	2.7t
6 France	2.5t
7 Italy	2.1t
8 Spain	1.4t
9 Canada	1.4t
10 Brazil	1.3t

Post Industrial Economy

Prior to WW2 the US economy was largely industrial based with most of the labour force employed in the manufacturing sector. Since the war the US economy has been transformed into a service based economy, 80% of US wealth is generated in the service sector. Wholesale trade, the manufacturing of consumer goods and retail comprise 65% of the services sector, i.e. the consumption of goods is what drives the US economy. The US over the last 30 years has become reliant on consumption and today is the world's largest consumer of many items. The US is the main engine for economic activity in the world and its huge level of consumption is responsible for most of the growth being experienced by China and India. With only 5% of the world's population the US consumes 25% of the world's oil and imports 9% of all goods manufactured outside the country, (the most in the world, 32% of this is consumer goods).

The manufacturing of goods and the labour behind them are being continually outsourced to cheaper locations, China has benefited from this immensely as it is now a factory for the US as 70% of its manufactured goods end up in the US. The US currently manufactures strategic items such as heavy machinery and items it considers of national interest and refuses to transfer such technology such as arms, aircrafts, motor vehicle parts, computers and telecommunications. The US consumer is now buying more from overseas than ever before, so much so that the US now has a huge trade imbalance with the rest of the world. Its trade deficit or the amount it imports more than it exports, with the rest of the world stood at a record $763.6 billion by the end of 2007.

The American consumer is at the centre of the US economy, their consumption is what drives the economy, their spending allows companies to continually expand production and any fall in spending would result in the complete breakdown of the US economy. A large chunk of consumer spending is on the purchase of homes and obtaining mortgages. Housing in turn fuels appliance sales, home furnishings and construction. In 1940 44% of US citizens owned their own homes, by 1960 62% of

National debt

1 US	12.8t
2 UK	11.5t
3 Germany	4.4t
4 France	4.3t
5 Italy	2.3t
6 Netherlands	2.2t
7 Spain	2.0t
8 Ireland	1.8t
9 Japan	1.4t

Americans owned their homes. Currently nearly 70% of all housing is owned by its constituents. The increase in home ownership has resulted in more and more US citizens becoming indebted, US household debt is $11.4 trillion (2006).[4]

This is a staggering figure considering 20% of US households now have more debt then assets. This debt represents enormous confidence in the future of the economy because the actual money doesn't exist. This debt is seven times the amount of dollars in circulation (M1 Money Supply), which is only $1.3 trillion (2007). Lenders assume the money will exist when it comes time for people to repay their debts. The importance of the consumer to consume to the US economy was outlined by Richard Robbins expert in anthropology in his award wining book *global problem and the culture of capitalism,* *'a couple of days after the al Qaeda operatives crashed two planes into the world trade centre on September 11th US congress members met to plan a message to the stunned public. "We've got to give people confidence to go back outside and go to work, buy things, go back to the stores, get ready for thanksgiving, get ready for Christmas,"* said one member of congress, echoing the message of the president *'get out'* he said *"and be active members of our society."* (CNN 2001). *The fact that after one of the most shocking events in US history government officials were urging citizens above all to shop and work is ample testimony the significance of consumption in the effective working of our economy and indeed for the whole society."*

Creating the Sub-prime Market

The Sub-prime mortgage market differs from the prime (primary) market as it comprises all those people who do not meet the criteria for a mortgage in the mainstream market.[5] The adoption of the Depository Institutions Deregulatory and Monetary Control Act in 1980 was part of the deregulation drive that eliminated many restrictions to lending, this resulted in loans reaching unprecedented levels which led to the mainstream mortgage market becoming saturated and reaching its peak of profitability. Those with patchy credit histories and of low income were turned away from mainstream mortgages at a time when the market was buoyant due to consumer spending and borrowing. The Sub-prime market was carved out after this point as 25% of the US population fell into this category and represented a market opportunity. Hence US lenders gave mortgages to people who had little means to pay for a mortgage and charged them a rate of interest much higher than the commercial rate due to the increased default risk. They issued these mortgages safe in the knowledge that if the buyer defaults, then they would be able to repossess the property, and sell in a buoyant property market. By the start of 2007, the sub-prime market was valued at more then $1.3 trillion.

Traditional banks stayed away from this risky market and instead remained focused on prime lending and questioned some of the business practices of sub-prime companies such as their aggressive lending and accounting practices. Between 1994 and 1997 the number of sub-prime lenders tripled, going from 70 to 210. Because such institutions were not banks they possessed no customer deposits and in order to expand many lenders turned to the stock market for funding. Companies such as Money Store, AMRESCO Inc, Dallas and Aames Financial Corporation, all raised capital through placing some of their companies on the stock market. Relatively young lenders such as Long Beach Financial Corporation; Irvine, California-based New Century Financial Corporation; Delta Funding Corporation; and Cityscape Financial all took their companies 100% public. By the end of 1997, the top 10 lenders accounted for 38% of all sub-prime lending.

The collapse of the Russian rouble and long term capital management in 1997 resulted in a number of foreclosures leading to the demise of six of the top 10 sub-prime lenders. This left an enormous vacuum in the sub-prime industry that resulted in a series of acquisitions by commercial banks such as Washington Mutual's acquisition of Long Beach Financial Corporation. Associates First Capital, the third-largest sub-prime originator at the time, was purchased by Citigroup Inc. In 2001, Chase Manhattan Mortgage Corporation acquired Advanta Mortgage

Corporation, the 16th-largest sub-prime lender at the time for $1 billion. In 2003, HSBC Finance Corporation acquired sub-prime powerhouse Household Finance, which had earned the rank of largest sub-prime lender in the two years prior to its acquisition by HSBC. Mortgage brokers did not lend their own money. There was no correlation between loan performance and compensation. Hence there were big financial incentives for selling complex, adjustable rate mortgages for such companies since this would earn higher commissions. In 2004 Mortgage brokers originated 68% of all residential loans, with sub-prime loans accounting for 43% of brokerages' total loans.

Securitisation

Most sub-prime lenders then invented another way of making money in a sector which was already highly risky. Many lenders wanted to ensure they didn't lose out at possible money making opportunities in the sub-prime market and developed a number of complex products; this was achieved by breaking down the value of the sub-prime mortgage market and various home loans into financial sausage meat - just as wholesome as the real world equivalent - and selling them on to other institutions. Debt was sold to a third party, who would then receive the loan repayments and pay a fee for this privilege. Thus debt becomes tradable just like a car. Hence the ability to securitize debt provided a way for risk to be sliced and diced and spread, thereby allowing more mortgages to be sold. Since 1994, the securitisation rate of sub-prime loans increased from 32% to over 77% of total sub-prime loans. This process effectively increased the number of financial institutions with a stake in the sub-prime mortgage market. This was allowed to happen due to the manner in which the original sub-prime loans were securitised.

Many institutions including mainstream Wall Street investment banks became owners of collateralised debt obligations (CDO's). These are bonds created by a process of deconstructing and re-engineering asset-backed securities. This essentially works by providing investors with access to the regular payments received from debt payers in return for paying to have access to the CDO as well as managements fees. Thus Wall Street investment banks made investments in the cash flows of the assets, rather than a direct investment in the underlying asset.

Many institutions also became owners of mortgage-backed securities (MBS) which were created out of the repackaging of sub-prime loans. In simple terms this is where a bank sells a set of debts as one product. In return for a fee the new holder of this debt obligation receives the regular loan repayments. In most cases such a debt forms part of a pool of mortgage based debts lumped together into a form of asset or bond, each with different degrees of risk attached to them. Thus owners of MBS's actually do not know the source of where the payments are coming from or even which sectors they're being exposed to. The MBS market is worth of $6 trillion currently, even more then US treasury Bonds. The difference between CDO's and MBS's is in the latter the property is placed as collateral.

In any event of a downturn in the housing market it would not only be the sub-prime providers who would lose out, but now all those who purchased collateral products would also be exposed.

Credit Ratings

Most debt carry ratings which indicate the amount of risk they entail, such a task is undertaken by credit rating agencies as an independent verification of credit-worthiness. The spotlight was originally thrown on the industry after the 2001 collapse of Enron - a firm built on securitisation as well as the role of credit rating agencies in the financial crash in the Asian financial crisis in 1997. Charlie McCreevy, EU internal market commissioner commented: "*What's the common denominator between Enron, Parmalat, special purpose vehicles, conduits and the like? They are off-balance sheet vehicles where the risk has theoretically gone with them: tooraloo, adiós.*"[6]

US home loans had been pooled and packaged into tradable securities by Wall Street banks, before being sold on to financial institutions around the world. As they were bought and sold, these mortgage-backed securities were valued according to the ratings given to them by the credit rating agencies. Credit agencies (dominated by the big three; Moody's, Standard & Poor's and Fitch) classify the risk of these repackaged securities according to their exposure to risky markets. CDO's were classified into tranches, the highest tranche was perceived to be very low risk and was often given an AAA rating – the same rating as high grade US Treasury Bonds. This is because in the event of default the first to incur the loss would be the lower tranches and not the top tier. The mathematical models and simulations that the banks relied upon did not predict a scenario where defaults would become so numerous that even the top tier AAA-rated tranches would be affected.

Sub-prime market collapse

As the housing sector continued to inflate due to the appetite for housing by Americans, the sub-prime sector continued to also grow. Commercial banks entered what they considered a buoyant market that could only rise, many Americans refinanced their homes by taking out second mortgages against the added value to use the funds for consumer spending. The first sign that the US housing bubble was in trouble was on the 2nd April 2007 when New Century Inc the largest sub-prime mortgage lender in the US declared bankruptcy due to the increasing number of defaults from borrowers. In the previous month 25 sub-prime lenders declared bankruptcy, announcing significant losses, with some putting themselves up for sale. This was in hindsight the beginning of the end.

The crisis then spread to the owners of collateralised debt who were now in the position where the payments they were promised from the debt they had purchased was being defaulted upon. By being owners of various complex products the constituent elements of such products resulted in many holders of such debt to sell other investments in order to balance losses incurred from exposure to the sub-prime sector or what is known as 'covering a position.' This second round of selling to shore up funds and meet brokerage margin requirements is what caused the collapse in share prices across the world in August 2007, with the market getting into a vicious circle of falling prices, leading to the further sales of shares to shore up losses. This type of behaviour is typical of a Capitalist market crash and is what caused world-wide share values to plummet. What made matters worse was many investors caught in this vicious spiral of declining prices did not just sell sub-prime and related products; they sold anything that could be sold. This is why share prices plummeted across the world and not just in those directly related to sub-prime mortgages.

International institutes who poured their money into the US housing sector realised they will not actually receive their money that they loaned out to investors as individual sub-prime mortgage holders were defaulting on mass on such loans this resulted in all those who took positions in the housing sector not being able to pay the institutes they borrowed money from. It was for this reason central banks across the world intervened in the global economy in an unprecedented manner providing large amounts of cash to ensure such banks and institutes did not go bankrupt. The European Central Bank, America's Federal Reserve and the Japanese and Australian central banks injected over $300 billion into the banking system within 48 hours in a bid to avert a financial crisis. They stepped in when banks, such as Sentinel, a large American investment house, stopped investors from withdrawing their money, spooked by sudden and unexpected losses from bad loans in the American mortgage market, other institutions followed suit and suspended normal lending. Intervention by the world's central banks in order to avert crisis cost them over $800 billion after only seven days.

Credit Crunch

Banks across the world fund the majority of their lending by borrowing from other banks or by raising money through the financial markets. The borrowing between banks is undertaken on a daily basis in order to balance their books. As the realisation dawned that sub-prime mortgage backed securities existed across the banking sector in the portfolios of banks and hedge funds around the world, from BNP Paribas to Bank of China. Many lenders stopped offering loans, some only offered loans at very high interest rates and most banks stopped lending to other banks to shore up their books. As no bank really knew how much each bank was exposed to the sub-prime crisis many refused to lend to other banks, this led to a credit crunch whereby those banks who made the majority of their loans from borrowed money found credit was drying up.

Major Sub-Prime losses
(As of June 2008)

Citigroup: $40.7bn
UBS: $38bn
Merrill Lynch: $31.7bn
HSBC: $15.6bn
Bank of America: $14.9bn
Morgan Stanley $12.6bn
Royal Bank of Scotland: $12bn
JP Morgan Chase: $9.7bn
Washington Mutual: $8.3bn
Deutsche Bank: $7.5bn
Wachovia: $7.3bn
Credit Agricole: $6.6bn
Credit Suisse: $6.3bn
Mizuho Financial $5.5bn
Bear Stearns: $3.2bn
Barclays: $3.2bn

Source: BBC

The first indication that this housing crisis was not just going to affect the US and would spread to the wider global economy was the effective collapse of Britain's Northern Rock. Northern Rock was the 5th largest mortgage lender in the UK and funded its lending by borrowing 80% from the financial markets. As the credit markets froze Northern Rock requested the Bank of England, as lender of last resort in the UK, for a liquidity support facility due to problems in raising funds in the money markets. This created a run on the bank as depositors lost all confidence in the bank leading to queues developing across the nation as depositors withdrew their cash in panic. The British government took the controversial decision to nationalise Northern Rock as its collapse would have inevitably spread to other banks as panic stricken depositors attempted to withdraw their savings - the whole banking sector would have collapsed.

A similar scenario occurred in March 2008 with Bear Stearns one of the world's largest investment banks as it was forced to write-off three of its investment funds in the sub-prime market. Bear Stearns's problems escalated when rumors spread about its liquidity crisis which in turn eroded investor confidence in the firm.

With the housing sector the driving engine for the US economy for the last decade; its collapse will have severe repercussions across the global economy as much of the world's banks placed their money through complex securitisation in the sub-prime market. With the US economy considered already in recession this will have world wide affects as the US economy drives the world economy due its huge consumption.

Oil: The Crude Facts

The US administration threw billions of dollars at its banking industry who suffered huge losses due to the housing market crash. As the credit crunch has matured most banks to shore up their losses moved into commodities. The price of oil crossed the $100 a barrel Mark in January 2008 – the highest since oil was first discovered over 100 years ago. The importance the black stuff plays in the modern economy is so crucial that slight changes in prices can affect economies. Today oil is used for numerous everyday products across the world, most commonly for powering combustion engines such as fuel oil, diesel oil and petrol. Oil is also used as fuel for heating and lighting (e.g. kerosene lamp). The petrochemicals industry produces many by-products such as plastics and lubricants. It also manufacturers solvents (alcohols) through oil, without which there would be no chemicals industry. The free flowing hydrocarbons allow many farming techniques and fertilizers. Hence small shifts in the price of oil have far reaching consequences. The fact oil prices shot through the roof at the same time the credit crunch matured has been publicly kept separate otherwise this would mean the housing bubble has been replaced by the commodities bubble.

Oil Past and Present

It was British naval power that brought Oil to the international scene. In 1882, Oil had little commercial interest. The development of the internal combustion engine had not yet revolutionised world industry. With Germany on the verge of shifting the global balance of power by developing its own oil propelled ship Britain began converting its naval fleet from bulky coal-fired propulsion to the new oil fuel.

WW1 brought to the international scene the importance of oil; it came to be seen globally as the key to military success. In an age of air warfare, mobile tank warfare, and naval warfare bulky coal-fired propulsion gave way to oil. Oil required only 30 minutes for ships to reach top speed compared to 4-9 hours when coal was used, battleships powered by coal emitted smoke which could be visible 10 kilometres away whilst oil had no tell-tale signs. The strategic advantage it gave was insurmountable and the British empires control of oil supplies become even more important given the fact that Great Britain had no oil supplies at the time. It was the capturing of the rich oil fields of Baku on the Caspian Sea denying vital supplies to Germany that resulted in the end of WW1 and German surrender. William Engdahl geopolitical expert outlined the importance of oil *'rarely discussed, however is the fact that the strategic geopolitical objectives of Britain well before 1914 included not merely the crushing defeat of Germany, but, through the conquest of war, the securing of unchallenged British control over the precious resource which by 1919, had proved itself as a strategic raw material of future economic development – petroleum. This was part of the 'great game' – the creation of a new global empire, whose hegemony would be unchallenged for the rest of the century, a British – led new world order.*[7] Britain and France concluded a secret oil bargain (Sykes–Picot agreement) agreeing in effect to monopolise the whole future output of Middle Eastern oil between them.

Oil Markets

Crude oil, also known as petroleum, is the world's most actively traded commodity. The largest markets are in London, New York and Singapore but crude oil and refined products - such as gasoline (petrol) and heating oil - are bought and sold all over the world. Crude oil comes in many varieties and qualities, depending on its specific gravity and sulphur content which depend on where it has been pumped from.

Because there are so many different varieties and grades of crude oil, buyers and sellers have found it easier to refer to a limited number of reference, or benchmark, crude oils. Other varieties are then priced around this, according to their quality. Brent is generally accepted to be the world benchmark, although sales volumes of Brent itself are far below those of Saudi Arabian crude oils. Brent is used to price 66% of the world's internationally traded crude oil supplies.

In the Gulf, Dubai crude is used as a benchmark to price sales of other regional crudes into Asia.

In the United States, the benchmark is West Texas Intermediate (WTI). This means that crude oil sales into the US are usually priced in relation to WTI. However, crude prices on the New York Mercantile Exchange (Nymex) generally refer to 'light, sweet crude.' This may be any of a number of US domestic or foreign crudes but all will have a specific gravity and sulphur content within a certain range.

Slightly confusingly, the Organisation of Petroleum Exporting Countries (OPEC) - a cartel of some of the world's leading producers - has its own reference. Known as the OPEC basket price, this is an average of seven - always the same seven - crudes. Six of these are produced by OPEC members while the seventh, Isthmus, is from Mexico. OPEC aims to control the amount of oil it pumps into the marketplace to keep the basket price within a predetermined range. In practice, the price differences between Brent, WTI and the OPEC basket are not large. Crude prices also correlate closely with each other.

OPEC's basket price is an average of the prices for:

Saudi Arabia's Arab Light
The United Arab Emirates's Dubai
Nigeria's Bonny Light
Algeria's Saharan Blend
Indonesia's Minas
Venezuela's Tia Juana Light
and Mexico's Isthmus.

Due to the nature of oil requiring extracting and refining participants commonly use futures contracts for delivery in the following month. In this type of transaction, the buyer agrees to take delivery and the seller agrees to provide a fixed amount of oil at a pre-arranged price at a specified location. Futures contracts are traded on regulated exchanges and are settled (paid) daily, based on their current value in the marketplace.

Oil price crisis

Although many experts continue to cite fundamentals are causing the price of oil to peak, this is no way explains the sudden hike in Oil prices, China and India's demand for oil has been known since the early 1990's as well as the worlds continuing appetite for oil, this in no way explains the sudden hike in prices. The price of oil has been on an upward trend since the beginning of the 21st century and the driving engine for this has been speculation.

With all the economies that have adopted Capitalism the financial sector is the driving engine which generates wealth. However wealth is not generated by producing real goods, goods which are made in factories, people are employed and then paid a wage. Most of the wealth generated in Capitalist nations is from the financial sector that doesn't actually produce anything but provide a service where one can bet on the future price of items. Capitalism was named after its most prominent aspect – Capital, the accumulation of capital and making money out of money is a lethal cocktail when greed and consumption are added – all these are the basic aims Capitalism attempts to achieve. In this endeavour Capitalism promotes the securitisation (trading) of any commodity whether it is real or imagined. Originally the stock market was created to bet on the future movement of share prices as well as the performance of a company. Thereafter the derivatives market was created which is a casino where betting takes place on the movement of the stock market and in the last two decades all commodities can be speculated upon.

On March 30th 1983 Nymex introduced futures in petroleum. That meant oil prices being fixed daily, determined by the give-and-take of Nymex traders, with buyers and sellers monitoring their computer screens worldwide. A futures contract is a promise to deliver a given quantity of a standardised commodity at a specified place and time in the future. It is a derivative, not the real thing. There are thousands of oil transactions daily, but few of these shipments are delivered. Instead, they are constantly re-traded, based on the market price of the moment. That is, the rights to a single barrel of oil are bought and sold many times over, with the profits or losses going to the traders and speculators. Given the current weakness in the world's stock markets, the falling value of the dollar, and the credit crunch caused by the sub-prime mortgage crisis in the US, speculators are putting their funds into such safe havens as gold and oil, spiking up their prices.

The large purchase of crude oil futures contracts by speculators have, in effect, created an additional demand for oil, driving up the price of oil for future delivery in the same manner that additional demand for contracts for the delivery of a physical barrel today drives up the price for oil on the spot market. As far as the market is concerned, the demand for a barrel of oil that results from the purchase of a futures contract by a speculator is just as real as the demand for a barrel that results from the purchase of a futures contract by a refiner or other user of petroleum.

Speculation Driving the Oil Crisis

A June 2006 US Senate Permanent Subcommittee on Investigations report on "The Role of Market Speculation in rising oil and gas prices" noted, "...

there is substantial evidence supporting the conclusion that the large amount of speculation in the current market has significantly increased prices" One geo-political expert confirmed *'Today 60% of crude oil price is pure speculation driven by large trader banks and hedge funds and with the development of unregulated international derivatives trading in oil futures over the past decade, the way has opened for the present speculative bubble in oil prices.'* [8]

Hence when speculators purchase a contract to buy oil at a given date, they do not actually buy or sell the oil but merely buy and sell the right and take the price differentials, physical oil is not traded. This is what has caused oil to reach astronomical levels; it has led to riots and inflated prices well beyond the common person.

This is why it is no surprise to see in a May 6th 2008 report from Reuters that Goldman Sachs announced oil could in fact be on the verge of another "super spike," possibly taking oil as high as $200 a barrel within the next six to 24 months. A large number of futures contracts where taken out as soon as the news went public. That headline, "$200 a barrel!" became the major news story on oil for the next two days. Many speculators followed with their bets?

A common strategy speculators are using desperate for more profitable investments amid the US sub-prime disaster is to take futures positions selling 'short'. By selling a commodity or any financial instrument short in essence this is betting on the price of the commodity or financial paper to fall. Short-sellers do not own anything they sell - they borrow them from pension funds and insurers. A common example is where; a hedge fund would borrow a million shares in Megabank for a fee. It would then sell those million shares at the prevailing market price of £8 a share, making £8 million in total. The hedge fund is betting and hoping that Megabank's share price would then fall. If it falls - to £4 a share the hedge fund then buys a million shares for £4m and returns them to the lender. This means that the hedge fund has banked a real cash profit of £4m. Lehman

24

Brothers, the investment bank, has estimated that fuel is 30% overpriced because of an influx of money into the oil market from investment funds. It believes that hot money accounts for between $20 to $30 of the recent increase in oil prices and that about $40 billion has been invested in the sector so far this year — equal to all the money pumped into oil last year.

Understanding the 'Fundamentals'

Most analysts and experts continue to interpret the price of oil price movements due to fundamentals – in the oil industry the fundamentals are factors that influence the supply of, and demand for, oil. Things such as the increasing demand

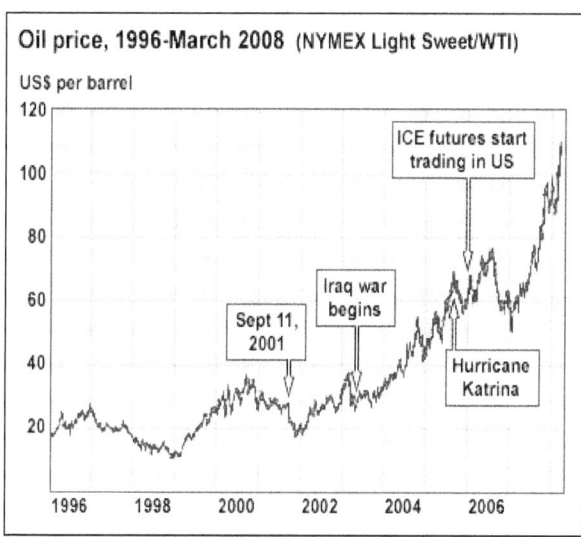

from China and India, as well as fears that a stand-off between the US and Iran could interrupt supplies are considered as having a bearing on oil prices. Alternatively, financial factors may be at work, such as a hedge fund having to sell a particular oil contract so it does not end up receiving a tanker-load of oil. However most fundamental information is not freely available. Mark Lewis from Energy Market Consultants explained in a BBC interview *"We really don't know what the fundamentals are doing at any point in time; the markets are looking for signals from the fundamentals. Some of them are irrelevant, some of them are wrong, some of them are meaningless, but they affect prices*

25

nevertheless." Sean Cronin, editor of Argus Global Markets explained *"When the New York oil price broke through $100 a barrel for the first time at the start of 2008, one of the factors cited as being behind it was the assassination of Benazir Bhutto in Pakistan on 27 December 2007, that didn't strike us as making any sense at the time."*

Hence there is a difference between the factors that raise oil prices because they affect sentiment and the ones that genuinely affect supply and demand for oil. This means hedge funds and the large investment banks in reality trade on rumour, not fact.

The speculation by hedge funds and Investment banks attempting to shore up their losses have been the main factors driving the oil crisis. There is however a number of other factors that have affected oil prices and will continue to shape the future geo-political scene

Refinery Capacity

A major factor which will add to the Oil crisis is the fact there are little plans to develop Oil refineries. An oil refinery is an industrial process plant where crude oil is processed and refined into more useful petroleum products, such as gasoline, diesel fuel, heating oil, kerosine, and liquefied petroleum gas

Oil refineries operate on a 'just-in-time' basis; this has affected the building of new refineries. The huge costs and the long lead times for building them affects decision making and as a result they are built only when they're needed. Both oil and gas prices were relatively low during the 1980's and 1990's; hence very few refineries were built. The surge in prices in the late 1990's was not expected to last hence refinery capacity did not increase - since to finance refineries a 25 year forecast of supply and demand is used. The rise of India and China happened too fast for an increase in refinery capacity; this is why over the past few years there have been refinery bottlenecks, which have contributed to the increased price in refined products such as gasoline, naphtha and jet fuel etc.

Although Oil production has continued to increase and although consumption is set to rise, for the last 30 years very few refineries have been built across the world. The region that has the largest oil reserves (61%) and pumps 31% of the world's oil – the Middle East, only refines 8% of it. 76% of the worlds oil is refined in regions with very little oil, but increasing demand for oil. The US refines 20% of the world's oil, whilst Europe refines 22% of the world's oil and the Far East refines 27% of the world's oil. Hence even though the Muslim world has the lions share of oil, in essence this is useless considering the inability to refine it, for this reason most of the oil is piped to the Far East and Europe to be refined, then the products are sold to the Muslim world. The primary motive behind the lack of US refinery new builds was due to the low price of oil, new refineries would have been an expensive venture eating too much into profits. In the 1980s and 1990s, the fashion for American refineries was not to build more, but to close existing ones. In 2001, Senator Ron Wyden authored a comprehensive report on the state of the US refining industry. He noted that between 1995 and 2001 there were a total of 24 refinery closures in the United States.

Wyden uncovered several memos and internal documents from major oil companies that charted the way that capacity in the US refining industry was reduced to maintain higher profits. In Europe not only have no new refineries been built for two decades but there are no plans to build any in the future. There are no firm expansions in refining capacity, not just in the US but in North America, South America and Europe. All of the expansions are in the Middle East and Asia, by the time they come online oil consumption would have drastically increased. This has added to the price hike of oil and will play a key role in the future.

Energy Geopolitics

Although the current crisis has in large part been due to speculators moving out of the sub-prime crisis and into commodities there are however a number of Geopolitical factors and trends that will affect oil prices in the future. The age of oil, produced its own technology, its balance of power, its own economy and its pattern of society. The future of energy security will play a key role in the global balance of power.

These factors are four:

1. **The Eastern threat -** The Middle East is gradually shifting from being a uni-polar region in which the US enjoys uncontested hegemony to a multi-polar region. The US will face more competition from China and India over access to Middle East oil. Soaring global demand for oil is being led by China's continuing economic boom and, to a lesser extent, by India's rapid economic expansion. Both are now increasingly competing with the US, the European Union and Japan for the lion's share of global oil production.

The demand for greater oil is affecting America's ability to pull itself out of its downturn and is creating inflation across the Western world. If China at any time in the future should develop its political will and ambition, it is in a relatively strong economic position to substantially weaken America.

2. **The Russian threat** - Russia, the leading producer of natural gas and one of the leading oil producers, is the global winner. The relationship between the European Union and Russia is now dominated by Russia and

will in the future make Europe dependent on Russian oil and gas. The oil shocks of the 1970s had different effects on different European countries. Britain had some North Sea oil and the prospect of more, as did Norway. Germany and France had little or no oil of their own. Differential shocks in the coming period of oil shortages will make it harder to maintain the Euro-zone.

Vladimir Putin has already used oil and gas as a diplomatic weapon against the European states, which have had to fall into line in June 2007 after making grandiose demands against Russia. Russia even made veiled threats against Britain during the famous spy poisoning case. Russia has also in the last year stopped supplying energy to its neighbours to quell dissent and ensure political allegiances.

Unlike China and India, Russia has a history of political strength and maturity, and the evidence over the last two years is that Russia has begun re-inventing itself as a regional power, after winning back Kazakhstan and Uzbekistan from the American grip and managing the stop the influence of the three revolutions in that region. America is becoming increasingly worried about the growing economic and political influence of Russia.

3. Oil and Petrodollars. One of the achievements of the US in the 1970's was to peg the price of oil to dollars. This meant that oil transactions are carried out in dollars only. This has allowed the US to maintain the dollar as the world premier currency and the currency of choice for foreign reserves.

However one of the key factors behind the rise in the price of oil is the devaluing of the dollar. Trading countries require more dollars for oil simply because the dollar is worth less - this would have increased the price of oil regardless of the increasing demand for it.

Today the European Union led by Britain and Germany are increasingly calling for pegging oil to the Euro; thereby stabilising the price of oil, and giving a stable revenue to oil producing countries. However, this severely impacts the dollar as a currency and if this was to happen would perpetuate America's economic crisis as the dollar would devalue even more.

4. The importance of the Middle East. Despite current supply shortages of oil around the world and the future restrictions, the importance of the Middle East, will not lessen. In fact it will become the most crucial area in the world.

This is because 61% of the world's oil reserves are in the Middle East. "Proved" oil reserves are those quantities of oil that geological information indicates can be with reasonable certainty recovered in the future from known reservoirs. Of the trillion barrels currently estimated only 39% are outside the Middle East. Today, 61% of global oil reserves are in the hands of Middle Eastern regimes: Saudi Arabia (22%), Iraq (11%), Iran (8%), UAE (9%), Kuwait (9%), and Libya (2%).

PROVED OIL RESERVES: 2006

61.5%   Saudi Arabia
21.9%

12%   9.7%
8.6%   5%   3.4%

Total: 1,208.2 billion barrels

- North America
- South and Central America
- Europe and Eurasia
- Middle East (Saudi Arabia 21.9%)
- Africa
- Asia Pacific

Proved reserves are those that the industry considers can be recovered in existing economies and operating conditions

SOURCE: BP

Currently of the 11 million barrels per day (mbd) the US imports 3 million barrels per day are from the Middle East. But in the years to come dependence on the Middle East is projected to increase by leaps and bounds. The reason is that reserves outside of the Middle East are being depleted at a much faster rate than those in the region. The overall reserves-to-production ratio - an indicator of how long proven reserves would last at current production rates – outside of the Middle East is about 15 years comparing to roughly 80 years in the Middle East. It is for this reason that George Bush said in April 2007, US dependence on overseas oil is a *"foreign tax on the American people."*

This is one of the most volatile regions in the world; and its importance will only grow stronger. The US is currently very worried about political developments in this region. A return of the Khilafah as predicted by several think tanks can potentially cripple America's economy, at a time where its political leverage is at its weakest since the end of the cold war.

The Oil price crisis once again highlights that the greed of speculators knows no bounds. It was greed that drove many banks to lend sub prime loans to individuals with no ability to repay the loans. It is again greed that is driving speculators to bet on Oil prices with no intention of actually purchasing the oil in order to make profits on the price differences – whatever the affect on the world. Such speculators drove the dot.com bubble, and then moved to the sub prime bubble once it burst and now they are pouring into the last remaining sector commodities – it is for this reason oil prices have reached astronomical levels, well beyond the reach of those who need it most. The Western world consumes 50% of the 21st century's most important resource, it produced less then a quarter of it. It is over consumption rather then China and India that are causing the crisis. The US specifically produced only 8% of the world's oil but consumes 25% of it.

Global Food Crisis

As the Credit crunch crisis matured another crisis hit the headlines. The soaring cost of food on the international markets raised the spectre of global inflation. The price of wheat alone has increased an astonishing 120% since August 2007, with the price of rice increasing by 75% since February 2008. With the Western world reeling

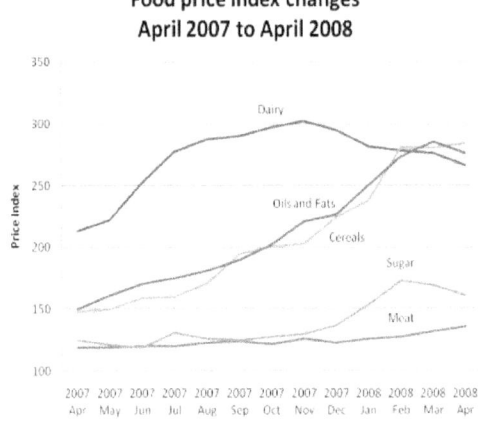

Food price index changes April 2007 to April 2008

Source: Food and Agriculture Organisation of the UN

from the collapse of the housing bubble crisis, the global food crisis would spell disaster due to food being essential for life. Western policy makers have refused to link the credit crunch with the food crisis as many investment banks and speculators moved out of the sub-prime sector and into commodities to shore up their losses and inflate another bubble to replace the housing bubble.

To deflect attention several reasons were put forward by Western politicians' and the mainstream Western media to explain the sudden price surge. The most commonly offered explanation was that food demand has increased globally over the last few years. In particular they cite the growing economies of China and India as having tightened global supplies of wheat, rice and corn; as they grow more affluent they are increasing their demand for meat based products for which these food stuffs are essential. They also cited poor harvests recently, particularly in Australia the worlds number two wheat producer, due to the ongoing drought the country is experiencing. Another reason put forward is that the wheat fungus striking parts of Eastern Africa, Yemen, Iran and Pakistan. These increases together with the increase in Corn price have been blamed on the growth in countries such as Brazil and America using land to grow Corn for bio-fuel derived Ethanol as a substitute for petrol. Thus, according to their argument, the land that could be used to grow wheat and rice is being lost.

Although food prices have been rising these reasons in no way explain the sudden surge in prices globally in such a short space of time. Despite all the claims about corn being used for bio-fuel, corn prices have only increased by a relative modest 31% as compared to the triple digit increases in wheat and rice prices in 2008. The populations of India and China have not increased to their present size in the space of a year. Neither have they grown proportionately affluent in the same space of time. China's economic growth has been underway for the last 30 years since it first started to reform its centrally controlled economy. India has also only introduced free market reforms since the early 1990s. Moreover global food production has increased twice as fast as the increase in the world population in the last 25 years. Last year the world produced a record 2.1 billion tonnes of grains, an increase of 5% on the year before. What is most shocking is that although a total 2.3 billion tonnes of food will be produced in 2008, only 1.5 billion is expected to be consumed.

This highlights globally the failure to make better use of existing food produce and to distribute it more efficiently and fairly. Whilst some food stock will inevitably be destroyed due to poor storage, the fact remains that man-made policies have encouraged poor use and wastefulness. The European Union has for many years given its farmers generous subsidies under its Common Agricultural Programme (CAP). The result has been that overproduction has taken place where excess 'food mountains' have been deliberately destroyed in the past. Where they have been have given to the poor in other parts of the world, they have been dumped at lower than the production cost, ruining local producers. America too provides its farmers generous subsidies. The result is that whilst the IMF and the World bank force third world countries to end any support they may give to their farming industry under the pretext of encouraging efficiency, market liberalisation and structural reforms, Western farmers derive a major portion of their income from government subsidies.

The sudden surge in food prices was due to speculators who have sought to diversify investments away from bonds, securities and mortgage related debt. After the credit crunch these were regarded as very bad investments. With money being diverted into buying stocks of wheat, corn and oil at some point in the future, using futures' contracts, this speculation is a self feeding cycle of frenzied increases.

In the same period Central Banks led by the Federal Reserve Bank of America pumped hundreds of billions of dollars into the Western banking system to save their banks and their financial system. This is one of the consequences that America has utilized ever since it de-linked it's currency from the Gold standard. Western governments chose to bail out these banks by printing and lending them money, an expansionist monetary policy, rather than risk the inevitable political consequences of these banks going bankrupt (As was seen with Bear Stearns and Northern Rock). The result of this increase in the global money supply has been global inflation. This in turn naturally forced up the prices of goods and services denominated in dollars as there was more dollars in circulation. As increase in money supply leads to the devaluation of the currency i.e. its purchasing power reduces.

All commodities including food are denominated and traded in dollars on the world's financial markets. With the amount of dollars circulating the financial markets soaring, the current crisis has been exasperated by the fact that most countries around the world, particularly poorer third world countries, hold foreign currency reserves mostly in dollars. As the purchasing power of the dollar has decreased, the worth of these dollar reserves has eroded, whilst at the same time food prices have increased. Countries which rely on importing food grains have been hit twice, in order for them to import food they would need to use their dollar reserves which have lost their purchasing power (i.e. they would need to use more dollars to buy the same amount of food), They would in all cases need to buy more dollars from the foreign exchange markets to by food which would mean they would need to sell their local currency to gain dollars (affecting their own exchange rate) and then buy food which is continually rising in price. As a result prices for food and other imported goods and services have increased in proportion to the inflationary effect. The sub-prime crisis has been exported to the poorest parts of the world by the US in order to save their financial system from ruin by literally printing more money.

The media has been concentrating on the immediate causes, which has avoided a discussion on the deeper issues and causes. A large chunk of land goes into producing products that are unnecessary or excessive in their production, such as tobacco and sugar. Also 80% of the world's production is consumed by the wealthiest 20%. The global food shortage in the coming months will further intensify as the increase in money supply slowly distributes itself through the global economy. As Western governments continue to pump money into their failed financial systems, the full effects of inflationary pressures are yet to be felt. With minimal regulation in Western countries, mainly as the result of close ties between politicians' and big business, the credit crunch has been replaced with another bubble. As a result the poor and vulnerable around the world have to suffer for the folly of Western bankers. This clearly shows how fragile Capitalism is as it can be easily manipulated by the financial markets, which has a tendency to create one disaster after the other.

Understanding the fragility of Capitalism

Like all previous crisis much literature has once again been written about the causes of current crisis. Many commentators, economists and cabinet ministers have again highlighted regulation, legislation and transparency. The current crisis shares many similarities with previous crisis that have occurred since the Great depression, there exists a whole host of specific factors inherent within Capitalism that caused the current credit crunch, food and oil crisis; such factors continue to plague the West and all those who have imitated the West. Without the removal of such factors that are inherent to Capitalism the world will continue to witness crashes and recessions. It is such underlying causes many Westerners refuse to address as this would be tantamount to questioning free market liberalism itself. Scrutinising the causes raises the prospect that a number of factors enshrined within Capitalism constantly cause such problems.

The Debt and Money Illusion

For the economies in the West to work consumers need to continually consume, this has been achieved by making sensual gratification the intellectual value for life. Companies could then fulfil this demand by producing the necessary goods which would be achieved by employing people. Such employees during the week are labour workers creating the very products that define life then during the weekends they become the consumers of such goods. This chain was then given various tools to ensure it keeps moving, the most important being debt.

In the 1950's there existed no credit cards in Britain; the US had introduced the world's first credit card in the 1950s with dramatic success, allowing people to buy things that could not have been imagined before for many people. However initially it was difficult to convince the public into accepting credit cards. A number of things were attempted to break through the resistance, this included launching credit Cards as "shopping card" initially. Such cards were aimed at women to show they could shop wherever and whenever they wanted. This also would have an effect of breaking the mould of the husband of the household owning the money flow. Bank's extended the payback period as it would be more profitable for the bank if people did not pay back in full immediately, but instead pay in smaller parts, because of the interest that would be added. By the 1960's when the emphasis in Britain was on getting rich and enjoying new fads, new inventions, and new ideas credit cards were well accepted with millions of customers, rather than being looked upon negatively as in previous decades.

Debt has come to play a central role in the mechanics of the Capitalist economy, from the funding of new start up's to the expansion plans of many multinational companies and also for many speculators as the means to invest on the stock market. In essence this practice is not inherently wrong. Individuals and companies will not have the necessary money for expensive expansion plans and would need to borrow to expand rather then wait years for profit accumulation. Banks in the last 300 years in the West developed to play a key part in the economy as they collected deposits and then used such wealth to issue loans.

It was Goldsmiths originally who developed fractional reserve banking as they realised the Gold deposited with them was never all withdrawn at any given time, they began the processes of lending more money then they had in their possession, this was achieved by issuing bills which promised gold on demand. As long as loans were not due at the same time and as long as depositors had confidence their money was sitting ready for them to withdraw and as long as every depositor didn't withdraw all there deposits at any given time then this illusionary system would reap handsome rewards for Goldsmiths – who are the forefathers of today's bankers.

The problem this creates can be seen with Britain's current dilemma. Because such money actually does not exist effectively banks are creating money and as a result of this the UK currently faces a crucial macroeconomic problem, that is with personal debt now more then £1.4 trillion (more then the actual economy) can this realistically be serviced (paid back) considering that the total supply of money and coins circulating in the economy on the last day of 2007 was only £52 billion.[9] How possibly can the UK's debt be repaid when the debt is actually more then the value of notes and coins in the economy? This shows that the actual money which has been given in debt by the banking industry actually doesn't exist. This debt represents enormous confidence in the future of the economy because the actual money doesn't exist; the banking industry simply assumes the money will exist when it comes for people to repay their debts. This means that although in the last decade the economy has grown enormously, this was largely through borrowing, hence debt has driven such economic growth. Such debt continued to grow funding growth in the different strata's of economy and now it has reached s a point were it has been realised that the debt may most likely not be repaid.

This practice is extremely fragile and it has been at the heart of the current crisis. Hedge funds and investment banks consider the loans they make as assets; they then recycled such debt at high velocity in a way creating turbo-debt. This works by companies and financial institutes borrowing money to invest, such investments will include a wide verity of different debt based products, this debt will then be used as a basis to borrow more money, hence £1 of debt can act as equity to finance more than £100 of credit. What this means is that borrowers in turn become lenders by effectively lending borrowed money! This releases a massive financial energy through a chain reaction of a tiny amount of initial equity, which never existed in the first place.

Hence fractional reserve banking creates illusionary money, which actually led to the explosive growth in the US sub-prime sector and the wider economy, because such factors are not real, confidence changes daily which is what causes the sharp rise and falls in the financial markets. As the publics pensions, bonds, deposits and interest rates are based upon the performance of the markets this causes consistent uncertainty and instability. The net effect of this is that such a negative effect on the financial markets and banking confidence will inevitably have an effect in the real economy. The key to this is expectations; companies will adjust their spending, investment and recruitment strategies according to what they expect to occur within the economy in the coming years. If they are expecting a collapse or significant downturn, they will begin to lay off staff (Citigroup announced job cuts of 9000 staff in April 2008)[10] and spend less. As more and more companies do this, we get a vicious circle of less spending, higher unemployment and eventually a recession.

A patch up created to deal with such a reality was the creation of Central Banks who would ensure the system remains stable and act as a lender of last resort if a bank faces a run. This is why the April 2008 £50 billion bail out package for banks organised by the bank of England and the government was considered the best of the worst options. What this has done has in fact promoted unscrupulous lending and predatory tactics by banks as they know they would be bailed out by their central bank if risky investment turned sour. This Moral hazard arises because Banks do not bear the full consequences of their actions, and therefore act much wildly than it otherwise would have if not insulated from risk if they were fully exposed to the risk. The Sub-prime sector was preying on the weak who have no means to buy a house, they were lent money at very high interest rates and when the sector turned sour central banks pumped in billions of dollars to shore up banks that made unscrupulous loans. This is also in direct contravention of the principal of free markets.

All current and future attempts to deal with economic crisis are destined to fail as banks will continue to use very small amounts of hard cash to lend large sums of money. In the pursuit of profits through interest banks are free to create money as the current global currencies are all fiat – i.e. they have no intrinsic value. The US today has used $1.3 trillion (M1) in notes and coins to lend over $11 trillion worldwide. With money today completely divorced from Gold and all intrinsic items there is nothing stopping the perpetual printing of money and for the Capitalist economy this is essential as it continues to fuel the Capitalist bubble.

The Twin Economy Dilemma

The development of Capitalism was the driving engine for the industrial revolution, until the 1960's the developed world was largely engaged in manufacturing, with most of the labour force employed in industry. Capitalist nations competed with each other in developing the latest technology in order to produce more with the finite resources available in the world. The economies in the West over the last 30 years have shifted their focus from industry to services to the point the service sector now represents over 80% of the US economy with the financial sector being the largest service. This development of the financial sector does not in any way manufacture goods or services but provides a new kind of service. Rather than work in the real world, participants gamble on what is going to happen in the real world – by betting on how businesses are performing and by betting on their profits. The financial sector is a parallel economy which exists alongside the real economy and produces nothing real. The real economy consists of housing, land and property, factories, cars and goods etc these are tangible goods which can be traded, leased and sold i.e. they are physical goods which are produced, people are employed to make them.

The financial economy consists of tradable paper which has financial values which rise and fall based upon the value people give to them. They have become so sophisticated that various products have been created which allow an investment in a paper with no real asset represented. This side of the economy is valued more then the real economy, the size of the worldwide bond market is estimated at $45 trillion. The size of the world's stock markets is estimated at $51 trillion. The world derivatives market has been estimated at $480 trillion, more then 30 times the size of the US economy and 12 times the size of the entire world economy.[11]

The existence of the financial markets has created dual economies in the West – the financial and the real economy. Cabinet ministers in charge of the economy are in effect managing two economies which require two distinct sets of policies; the best example of this is the dilemma the UK currently faces. The UK has been hit hard by the credit crunch and the knock on affects of this is their is a real possibility the UK will go into recession in 2009, a recession is where the economy actually shrinks rather then grow as there is less spending by both companies and individuals. This has the knock on affect of companies making redundancies as they cut back production, which means individuals will have no income (as they are out of work) hence they will scale back their spending. At the same time we are witnessing a situation in the real economy which has now reached boiling point, the easy availability of credit for the last decade led to many individuals to fund their lifestyles through debt which has now resulted in a possible explosion in inflation which would have far reaching consequences with the prospects of a recession. To contain inflation interest rates would need to rise – this would make saving attractive rather then spending and as most people have a mortgage in the UK, people would need to pay more each month for their mortgages and loans hence they will cut their spending as their mortgage will eat further into their incomes. However with the very real prospect of a recession this would be a disastrous policy as people need to spend rather then cut their spending because economic activity needs to be stimulated in order to avoid a recession. Hence a problem created in the financial economy is being borne in the real economy and the solution to the problem created by the financial economy would be disastrous for the real economy. So rather than lowering inflation by increasing interest rates, we are seeing that the strategy to control inflation is remaining unchecked, due to the condition of the financial markets; risking a recession.

With the financial sector representing the largest segment in the economies of the West it has also caused prices to become completely detached from the fundamentals of supply and demand. Experts continue to argue that the current commodities boom is driven by profound and lasting changes in global supply and demand: China's insatiable appetite for food and energy, geopolitical conflicts in the Middle East, the peaking of global oil reserves, droughts caused by global warming and so on. However these is no way explain whether the oil prices will soon jump to $200, or why food has because so expensive in the space of a few months.

The "fundamentals" are becoming more and more irrelevant, the oil markets didn't suddenly discover China's oil demand in 2007, however oil prices have doubled since last August 2007. China's demand for oil has decelerated. In 2004 China was consuming an extra 900 000 barrels a day; in 2007 it was consuming just an extra 300 000 mbd. In the same period global demand growth has also slowed from 3.6 mbd to 0.7 mbd. As a result, the increase in global demand growth in 2008 is well below the 2007 rate. The financial sector trades on rumor not 'facts' or 'fundamentals this is why it is possible for commodities to be rising in price even when there is no demand for them.

Britain along with the US is widely viewed as post-industrial economies that have abandoned manufacturing in favour of consumption and "hyper-finance." The financial sector now outstrips the real economy manifolds and this has resulted in this sector influencing government policy across the western world. Whilst Enron was left to collapse the US Federal Reserve pumped over $250 billion into the financial markets within 48 hours after the markets fell in August 2007. By having twin economies; banks, hedge funds and speculators were able to make risky investments without having to worry about the affects of their decisions in the real economy. Such type of economies allow for a strata of society to use the deposits of society to make risky investments and enjoy the proceeds, whilst if things go wrong society would pick up the burden of inflation and recession.

The Boom and Bust Virus

The global commodities and credit crisis has once again raised the debate of why a 'bubble' (speculation) was allowed to continually grow to unsustainable proportions and why such a 'boom and bust' phenomena has become such a common occurrence in the West? The boom and bust or economic cycle is considered inseparable from Capitalism and part of modern 21st century life. However the affects of busts, collapses and downturns have far reaching consequences and as previous instances have shown the masses suffer horrendously.

The cause of the boom and bust cycle and its consequences are a direct result of the ideal Capitalism attempts to achieve with the economy, and that is of perpetual economic growth. Based upon this Capitalist economies are structured towards production and consumers will buy what is produced. The current crisis highlights this very clearly as investors and consumers alike are continually bombarded with information on what to buy and the next big boom. Like the UK, the US experienced economic growth that was fuelled by the expansion of personal debt, which in turn was fuelled by the high price of real estate. As the cost of housing rose, house owners began increasingly taking out personal debt, offering equity on their homes as collateral. This process of effectively re-mortgaging homes in order to fund an extravagant lifestyle has been a nation wide phenomenon for the US. As long as house prices continued to rise, consumers will be able to take out more debt against the value of their homes. This practice has been evolving since the 1990's, and we now have a situation where house prices are so high that they have outstripped salaries by several times. The situation reached a dangerous threshold where such debt was struggling to be serviced and houses were increasingly too expensive to be bought by people.

This situation was never sustainable. House prices have been rising not because of demand but due to speculation. Speculators are seeking to make profits by buying houses, hoarding them and selling them on for a higher price. This process of speculation is fuelled entirely by the confidence speculators have that house prices will continue to rise. On top of this they are funding this speculation by borrowing money.

As it is confidence that formed the basis of the economic boom being experienced by Western economies, it is no wonder that they are subject to uncertainty. This confidence could be shattered if enough people feel that economic indicators in major economies in the world are not looking good. This is what effectively occurred in August 2007 with panic selling on the world's financial markets. What we witnessed was both individuals and large banks were no longer able to finance their debts. If enough people perceived this to be so, the housing market will begin to be flooded with people trying to quickly cash in on their homes before prices start to crash. As more homes come on to the market, a downward spiral is created as the extra supply of housing on the market forces prices down, causing yet more people to panic and try to sell their houses which continues the cycle. This would have a knock on effect on the rest of the economy, which so heavily relies on this perceived confidence in the real estate market, which would then impact the world who rely on the US economy for most of their exports. This is exactly what has happened since August 2007.

As speculators pulled their money out of the housing sector this resulted in the value of house prices collapsing and all those who have mortgages will end up repaying well above the value of the property.

This scenario is similar to what lead to the great depression where the West witnessed complete economic breakdown. The problem began in the US after WW1 when the US began a period of isolation. The US concentrated on individualism, which was termed the American dream promoting the acquiring of goods as the means to happiness. Demand was manufactured by new marketing methods and the US witnessed an unprecedented level of economic growth, were many individuals become millionaire's overnight due to the huge increase in national production. However by 1927 the US public was purchasing goods with more and more borrowed money even the rise in the Stock Exchange during the 1920's was by borrowed money. This new wealth was not distributed in an evenly manner and cracks begun to appear in 1927. The problem lied in the fact that the huge increase in wealth was in the hands of a few with the vast majority not actually receiving the fruits of national wealth and were using more and more borrowed money to keep pace with the boom. The US under the leadership of Herbert Hoover in order to stimulate the Economy after WW1 manufactured demand by making the acquiring of consumer goods the ultimate level of pleasure the result of this was a huge increase in the purchase of consumer and luxury goods. This ensured companies increased production gradually and the US population would find employment. However, Most of this lavish lifestyle was being funded by debt and over a course of 7 years more and more Americans used debt to fund their lifestyles. In 1927 most Americans began to feel the squeeze and began to use their salaries to pay for the debt they had accumulated. The result of this was eventually shop shelves remained stocked with consumer items as a large chunk of the populations disposable income was being used to service their accumulated debt. This had a knock on affect to other sections of the economy as suppliers to department stores no longer received orders, manufacturers stopped receiving orders from suppliers and then manufactures were forced to lay staff off. The first manifestation of Capitalism un-sustainability was the October 27th 1929 Stock Market crash on this single day 87% of the markets value was wiped off - the capitalist system's unsustainable bubble had burst.

As each segment of the capitalist economy relies on the proceeding segment the system is built upon creating artificial needs to keep consumers purchasing more and more goods to keep the main segment (catalyst) going. This is why the developed world witnesses regular recessions when enough people have spent beyond their means there would inevitably be a reduction in aggregate spending by consumers as a large chunk of disposable income is now used to service debt, this cycle of spending – increase in production – more jobs – purchasing more goods is never sustainable and has to end somewhere.

The financial markets have become so divorced from the real economy purchasing shares in a company is no longer undertaken to receive a dividend but to take advantage of inflated price rises. This has led to speculation of gigantic proportions to take place including bets on the collapse of economies. Currency speculators took huge positions on the currencies of the tiger economies in 1997, they were betting on the currencies collapsing and in collaboration with other investment houses pulled their money out of South East Asian Assets, shares, real estate and currency leading to a collapse in region. Hedge funds made billions from the misery of millions. This crisis came to be known as the Asian financial crisis.

Iceland in April 2008 was on the receiving end of speculative attacks by currency speculators who wanted to make money on the future collapse of the Icelandic Krona. Although Icelandic banks had sufficient deposits and in the past have been seen as a stable place to invest, speculators spread false rumors to create fears of a banking crisis in the country in order to profit from short positions (bets) on the Icelandic Krona. This was similar to rumors spread by some speculators that Britain's largest mortgage lender HBOS was on the verge of collapse in March 2008. This process is the same as betting shops across the world where individuals bet on the outcome of a Football match or who will score first. In the financial world you are betting on the outcome of economic decisions.

Bear sterns also found itself on the receiving end of speculator activity which eventually lead to its collapse. Hedge funds spread rumors about its liquidity crisis so they could bet on its eventual demise; this in turn eroded investor confidence in the firm. Securities and Exchange Commission Chairman Christopher Cox confirmed this in a letter to the firm in March 2008 *'the collapse of Bear Stearns was due to a lack of confidence, not a lack of capital. Notwithstanding that Bear Stearns continued to have high quality collateral to provide as security for borrowings, market counterparties became less willing to enter into collateralized funding arrangements with Bear Stearns.'* He confirmed *'Bear Stearns' liquidity pool started at $18.1 billion on March 10th 2008 and then plummeted to $2 billion on March 13th 2008. Ultimately market rumors about Bear Stearns' difficulties became self-fulfilling.*[42]

These examples show speculation plays a central role in economic growth and it is this which creates a bubble waiting to burst. Speculation is enshrined in Capitalism, even at the expense and wellbeing of society.

Consumption + Greed = Capitalism

The consumer is essential for Capitalism. Not only must consumers buy, they must buy more every year, and still more the year after that. Without perpetual consumption, the economy would either decline or collapse. The sign of a healthy national economy is measured by the Gross Domestic Product (GDP), and GDP is a measure of the quantity of goods and services people consume.

In the UK 1 million people are considered to have a shopping addiction; in the US, it is 5 million. Dr. Lorrin Koran, a professor of psychiatry at Stanford University and expert in behavioural Science said *"Its not just individuals who are addicted to shopping, our economy is too. Personal spending now plays a bigger and bigger role in keeping the modern economy going. And when things start going wrong, there is no magic pill. Governments rely on consumers to bail them out. There was a very real fear that September 11 would cause spenders to lose confidence and plunge the world into recession. Keeping people spending has become the top economic priority."*[13]

With consumption playing such a key role in the functioning of Capitalism, people have come to be symbolised by what they wear, eat and drive. Hence sensual gratification has become life's aim and with the dwindling world resources and ever increasing numbers competing for sensual gratification greed has come to characterise Capitalist societies. Capitalism believes if individuals in society pursue their self-interests then the right resources are produced for those who want them and this is the best way to allocate resources.

Today self interest (greed) is considered a necessary trait for the 21st century individual; its corruption can now be seen across society. Greed is the motivation that led to predatory mortgage brokers selling mortgages to people that have no way in paying it back, and then increasing the rates of interest until the buyer defaults. Greed was also the motivation that led the credit ratings agencies to rate the investments less risky than they really were, and also to conceal that the risk was based on sub-prime mortgage debt. Hedge funds demonstrated greed in the way they seek to provide astonishing returns to their customers, and greed is the motivation even for individual shareholders that want to capitalise on the falling share prices across the economy, even though it can lead to problems for thousands of people. The effect of this is devastating; since each element within society puts their benefit before ethics and morals, this is why we have a situation where even if the effect of an investment decisions can lead to a downturn in the economy, companies are prepared to make those decisions anyway.

- It was outright greed that drove the Western world to colonialise Africa and the Middle East in order to transfer the natural and mineral resources to the home nation, enslaving the indigenous population. The developed world can consume precisely because others are poor. This is why the situation of the majority of the world's population is abject poverty.

- It is greed by the Multinational pharmaceutical companies who neglect the diseases present in the third world, not because the science is impossible but because there is no market. There is a market for anti ageing, wrinkle elimination and Viagra. Pharmaceutical companies believe they would not make sufficient return on research investment, even if a cure saves the lives of millions.

- The Global food crisis has once again highlighted the greed of the Capitalist West. The situation of the majority of the world's people is one of abject poverty and misery. 3 billion in the world live on fewer than two dollars a day. From amongst them 1.3 billion have no access to clean water; 3 billion have no access to sanitation and 2 billion have no access to electricity. The world is standing on the brink of disaster as it is running out of food due apparently to the rate of population growth in the third world over the last century. The Capitalist West in reality over consumes and its greed here has left it to feed off the third world. The Industrialised West consume 81% of all that is manufactured in the world, although the third world has most of the resources and minerals needed to manufacture the worlds goods, the third world only consumes 3.6%. The Western world consumes 50% of the 21st century's most important resource; oil, it produced less then a quarter of it. The US currently with only 4% of the world's population, consumes 25% of the world's resources. For the first time in human history, the number of overweight (obese) people rivals the number of underweight people.[14] In the United States, 55% of adults are overweight by international standards. This is why Liposuction is now the leading form of cosmetic surgery in the United States, over 400 000 operations are undertaken every year.

- The cause of the global food crisis exposes how entrenched greed has become in the West.
  The global food crisis is the consequence of America's attempt to inflate its way out of market failure. The rocketing price of wheat, soya beans, sugar, coffee etc is all part of the credit crisis which has caused panic in the financial markets and encouraged speculators to take their money out of risky mortgage bonds and shaky equities and put them into commodities as 'stores of value,' i.e. Western banks are exporting their debts to the third world. The phenomenal increases in food prices are only in part a consequence of climate change and population. The current unprecedented crisis has been the result of speculation and the

collapse in the value of the dollar. This has been encouraged by the US Federal Reserve, who is trying to ignite another asset bubble to replace the real estate and dotcom bubbles which burst in spectacular fashion.

Speculators, who are desperate for quick returns to shore up their sub-prime losses, are taking trillions of dollars out of private equity and financial derivatives and are sinking them into food and raw materials - speculators are even placing their bets on water prices. This has resulted in an astronomical rise in food prices across the world which is hitting the third world the hardest, which apart from living on less then $2 a day rely on such basic foodstuffs. The global food crisis shows Capitalisms creates a mindset that makes one greedy for more and more even if the third world starves. Speculators piled into telecom stocks in the 1980's creating a bubble, and then internet stocks in the 1990s as the boom in dotcoms got under way. Then they shifted into real estate sub-prime mortgages. Now, with the collapse of the property bubble across the world, speculators are pouring into the only place left – food and commodities.

- Greed played a central role in the largest corporate bankruptcies in US. The collapse of Enron Corporation (the worlds dominant energy trader) in 2001, leading to the demise of Arthur Anderson (the largest accounting firm in the world at the time) and the subsequent collapse of WorldCom (the 2nd largest Telecom company in the US at the time) highlighted how greedy executives attempted to make a quick dollar by whatever means necessary.

In order for Enron executives to continue paying themselves large bonuses and be able to give large payments to their shareholders Enron created offshore entities who would be transferred their losses which would then no longer be shown on Enron's balance sheet. Enron's executives performed financial deception to create the illusion of billions in profits while the company was actually losing money. This practice drove up their stock price to new levels, at which point the executives began to work on insider information and trade millions of dollars worth of Enron stock. The executives and insiders at Enron knew about the offshore accounts that were hiding losses for the company; however shareholders knew nothing of this fraud. Arthur Anderson audited their accounts and gave their approval at the state of Enron's books. The fraud become public when Enron announced a $1 billion loss in October 2001 and with the loss of investor confidence and accusations of fraud and subsequent regulatory investigations revealed over $9 billion losses. On November 30th 2001 Enron filed for bankruptcy, its workers were told to pack up their belongings and were given 30 minutes to vacate the head office. 4,000 employees lost their jobs, savings, children's college funds and pensions.

- In the pursuit of profits Arthur Anderson was prepared to lie about Enron's accounts; The company was even convicted of obstruction of justice for shredding documents related to its audit of Enron. This resulted in the firm losing all of its clients when it was indicted, and there are over 100 civil suits pending against the firm related to its audits of Enron and other companies. Arthur Anderson eventually voluntarily surrendered its right to practice in August 2002. The Andersen indictment also put a spotlight on its faulty audits of other companies which subsequently caused the largest bankruptcy in US history.

- WorldCom was created through a merger in 1998 and quickly rose to become the largest Telecoms Company in the US after AT&T. Bernard Ebbers chief executive officer became very wealthy from the rising price of his holdings in WorldCom's stock, which he brought with substantial debt. WorldCom's growth strategy suffered a serious blow when it was forced to abandon its proposed merger with Sprint in late 2000, this lead to huge fall in WorldCom's stock. Ebbers came under increasing pressure from banks to cover margin calls on his WorldCom stock that he used as collateral to finance his timber and yachting interests. WorldCom's board provided Ebbers with corporate loans and guarantees in excess of $400 million to avoid the selling of substantial WorldCom stock as its share price would collapse. This strategy ultimately failed and Ebbers was ousted as CEO in April 2002 and was replaced. The new CEO used fraudulent accounting methods to mask WorldCom's declining financial condition by painting a false picture of financial growth and profitability to prop up the price of WorldCom's stock.

  WorldCom's internal audit department uncovered approximately $3.8 billion of the fraud in June 2002 during a routine examination of the companies' books. Shortly thereafter Arthur Andersen withdrew its audit opinion for 2001 which resulted in the US Securities and Exchange Commission (SEC) launching an investigation into the company. By the end of 2003, it was estimated that the company's total assets had been inflated by around $11 billion and on July 21st 2002 WorldCom filled for bankruptcy, the largest in US history.

- Throughout the 1990's it was greed that led many Western companies to relocate production operations abroad to cheaper nations with lax laws, very small pay and where labourers work for over 12 hours a day. Because of extensive labour laws in the West, the minimum wage and the rights employees have in the workplace; this practice was considered eating too much into company profits. An example of this is Gap Inc, who was taken to court by sweatshop workers in Saipan on allegations of forcing workers to work 'off the clock' hours, where workers were not paid for overtime, unsafe working conditions and forced abortions.

Capitalism creates a mindset that only cares for making profits however they are made. Very little attention is paid to the suffering and misery that such actions can cause, and perversely we have a situation where companies prey on the suffering of the people. In the search for profits multinational companies forcibly remove populations, pollute the atmosphere and experiment on host populations from Nigeria to Indonesia. Even in Western countries companies ruthlessly prey on the consumerism of the masses. The sub-prime housing sector is exactly that, it is an act of exploitation as companies offer big loans to people with bad credit histories as long as they offer their homes as collateral! Since the targeted people are the most likely to have a spending problem, these loan companies will then repossess the house and sell it to obtain their money plus the extortionate rate of interest added on top.

The principal problem here is that this motivation is seen as a virtue. Greed is good and necessary for modern life. Hence greed is a systematic problem; i.e. it is enshrined in Capitalism. No amount of regulation or legislation can deal with this as it is part of the mentality of the West i.e. it comes directly from the Capitalist belief.

The Globalisation Curse

Since the advent of Capitalism free markets and free trade has continued to be spread as the only way for economies to function. In the late 20th century such ideas where given further impetus through the call of Globalisation and many nations where given the IMF and World Bank structural adjustment treatment. However such ideas are what has allowed an essentially US problem to spread to the world. The last two decades has seen many economies being liberalised (opened) due to globalisation and many suffered from catastrophic crisis. It is also believed the best way to distribute wealth around the economy is to remove all government intervention allowing the forces of supply and demand in a free market to distribute wealth. This ideal has proven to be false for the last 200 hundred years and a number of examples clearly outline this:

- Argentina was considered by the IMF to be a model country in its compliance to policy proposals by the Bretton Woods institutions; however it experienced a catastrophic economic crisis in 2001, which was caused by IMF-induced budget restrictions — which undercut the government's ability to sustain national infrastructure in crucial areas such as health, education, and security. The IMF intervened to ensure its loans would be repaid and enforced a set of liberal reforms in order that Argentina integrates into the global economy. Argentina was ordered to structurally change its economy to concentrate on exports in order to raise enough money to pay off their debts. It was also forced to remove all barriers to foreign trade and foreign capital. What Argentina witnessed was a speculative attack on its currency by large finance houses who wanted to make a killing on the peso; this was easily achieved as Argentina had removed all restrictions on capital flight in order to be part of the globalisation movement. Argentina was unable to stop capital flight as such tools where abandoned on behest of the IMF. In December 2001 on the verge of economic meltdown Argentina defaulted on its $93 billion debt.

- The fall of communism in 1990 and the break-up of the Soviet Union represented a wonderful opportunity for capitalist institutes to transform a huge centralist economy to a market orientated one. A total of $129 billion poured into Russia with the IMF and the World Bank implementing a number of its development schemes. The Russian economy was opened to foreign investment and industry was sold to foreigners leaving the country vulnerable to swings in world prices. In 1997 due to a loss on confidence in Russia speculators begun to withdraw their money and Russia couldn't even defend itself as liberalisation required there to be no restrictions on capital flow. The crisis raised poverty from 2 million to 60 million, a 3000% increase. UNICEF noted that this resulted in 500,000 'extra' deaths per year. Russia is a clear example that globalisation directly allowed the crisis to reach the peak it did.

- By 1997, Asia attracted almost half of total capital inflow to developing countries. The economies of Southeast Asia maintained high interest rates attractive to foreign investors looking for a high rate of return. As a result the region's economies received a large inflow of hot money and experienced a dramatic run-up in asset prices. At the same time, the regional economies of Thailand, Malaysia, Indonesia, the Philippines, Singapore, and South Korea experienced high growth rates, 8-12% GDP, in the late 1980s and early 1990s. This achievement was broadly acclaimed by economic institutions including the IMF and World Bank, as the Asian economic miracle. But then the story turned sour.

From 1985 to 1995, Thailand's economy grew at an average of 9% per year. In May 1997, the Thai baht was hit by massive speculative attacks as investors tried to cash in on their money. By withdrawing their cash in large sums the currency collapsed, this set of a domino affect where financers lost confidence in the region and began moving their money out in large sums leading to the infamous Asian financial crisis. The only country in the region to survive the fall out was Malaysia as it was not under the control of the IMF's structural adjustment program and had placed restrictions on capital withdrawal from its country which meant speculators could not withdraw in large numbers at will. The rest of the region left their economies open hence they were unable to do anything when speculators withdrew their capital, thus proving free markets was the problem. This problem was aptly encapsulated by Economic expert Paul Krugman of Princeton University *"As long as capital flows freely, nations will be vulnerable to self-fulfilling speculative attacks, and policymakers will be forced to play the confidence game. And so we come to the question of whether capital should really be allowed to flow so freely."*[15]

- Turkey in 2001 faced the brunt of the IMF's globalisation policies as US investors withdrew large amounts of their capital. Turkey was ordered to peg its currency to the US dollar, a peg works on the basis that a currency is linked to another currency by ensuring the exchange rate remains within agreed bands on the open market. If the currency moves out of the bands then the government would literally sell or buy currency to bring it within the bands. As investors scrambled to buy foreign currency, the Turkish central bank reached the point where it could no longer support the exchange rate, hence it abandoned it and was about to default on its loans. The peg to the dollar was realistically never sustainable and by liberalising the economy it was only a matter of time before foreign investors cashed in and moved out. The currency peg, which controlled the movements of the lira, was the centrepiece of the IMF-backed financial reform package designed for Turkey. By removing restrictions on capital flight Turkey was unable to defend itself. Akyüz and Boratav, well-known economists from Turkey (Akyüz is Director of the UNCTAD Division on Globalisation and Development Strategies and Boratav is Professor of Economics at the University of Ankara) at the time commented, **"In many respects the Turkish economy today is in a worse shape than it was on the eve of the December 1999 stabilization programme."** They went on **"the policies advocated were based on a poor diagnosis of economic conditions in the country and the Fund was experimenting with programmes that lacked sound theoretical underpinnings."**[16]

Capitalism is geared completely towards wealth creation and leaves the allocation of such wealth to the market; this has resulted in huge wealth disparities in the developed world and is its biggest failure. Capitalist philosophy believes the best way to distribute wealth around the economy is to leave allocation to the market as through the interplay of supply and demand wealth will trickle down to all those who want it.

The US generated $13 trillion in 2006; however US statistics show the majority of this wealth went to a minority of the population. 13% of US population earned 53% of the income generated in 2006; this means 87% of the population shared in only 42% of the income,[17] it is for this reason 37 million Americans live below the poverty line. This is also why the national debt is $9.1 trillion (2007), US citizens are funding their lifestyles by borrowed money, the new wealth is only held by a select few.

The US suffers from a huge trade deficit and debt problem, due to globalisation, free markets and the US dollar the US has been able transfer its debts abroad. If the US dollar ceases to be the reserve currency and nation's restricted trade and finance the American economy would not be sustainable. As a result US economic problems spread across the world due to globalisation.

The distribution of wealth in the UK is even more lopsided; in 2006 93% of the wealth generated was held by just half of the population. The nations wealthiest 1% owned 25% of the nation's wealth. [18] Thus although the nations wealth has increased in the last decade the majority of the population never saw this wealth, they were forced to borrow and this has lead to consumer debt to exceed the nations wealth.

There should be no doubt Capitalism caused the credit crunch crisis and the food and Oil crisis and will continue to cause the periodic crash, depression, collapse and recession as its fragile nature is to continually create a speculative bubble which drives the economy to continually produce. As long as the public consume and are duped to continually consume every boom will be followed by a bust and with the ability of banks and governments to perpetually print money no amount of regulation, legislation, transparency and accounting rules can solve this as this is the Capitalist ideology.

The Islamic Economy

In origin every economic system attempts to address the same issues, namely how to utilise the available resources in order to satisfy the needs of the people. Hence every economic system would define the individual and the needs that require satisfaction. **How such resources are allocated is where each economic system differs.** Hence Capitalism distributes resources, goods and services by leaving allocation to the market, where prices are set according to supply and demand. Whilst Socialism allocates resources centrally according to the principal *'each according to his ability, and each according to his needs'*. All economic systems have defined descriptions of ownership and how the interplay of supply and demand create prices and these definitions allow for the derivation of rules for buying, selling, investments, employment and company structures.

The Islamic economic system is essentially composed of certain general principals, coupled with a set of derived rules. This System then provides the framework for addressing the diverse economic issues found within the society, which can vary in terms of scope, as it can be very specific to certain individuals and groups or very general such that it affects the entire society. So the framework provides these solutions for the general and detailed issues relating to all spheres of economic activity, such as buying, selling, investing, loans, currency, work, company structures, import and export and contract laws.

Islam makes a distinction between the economic system and economic science. This is because there is a fundamental difference between the method of production of goods and services (economic science) and the manner of their distribution (economic system). The production of goods and services follow no particular viewpoint in life. An industrial complex is neither Capitalist, Islamic or Communist, it is universal. Questions as to how processes can be made more technological, how various methods and machinery can improve productivity and how inventions can improve the process of manufacturing do not follow any specific viewpoint in life.

This means basic facts on productivity and manufacturing (economic science) remain the same irrespective of belief or location. This is similar to scientific facts. These are the same whether in China or the US because they are not influenced by any belief. They are questions based upon the reality i.e. understanding the reality at hand leads one to a conclusion. So the fact inflation occurs when there is too much money chasing too few goods does not change if one is a Christian or if an atheist becomes Muslim, or if one move's from China to the US.

The manner of distribution of resources, how goods and services should be given to the public, whether they should go to the rich or the orphans, aristocracy or the landlords etc is not a discussion based upon the reality. That which defines how to distribute the wealth, how to possess it, and how to spend or dispose of it (economic system) can never be taken from the reality as the reality does not explain this. The goods and what they are made of do not manifest themselves with answers of who they should go to. Neither is there any evidence from looking purely at the goods and services themselves of a way of deciding how they should be distributed. Therefore the answer must emanate from some point external to the reality i.e. a belief system or ideology.

Islam has a completely different philosophy for the economy which results in a very different society to a Capitalist one. This chapter will not focus on the entire economic system, but some aspects that will solve the aforementioned problems we have witnessed. The economic policy in Islam or the overall direction of the Islamic economic system is to secure the satisfaction of all basic needs for every individual completely, and to enable them to satisfy their luxuries as much as possible. So from this perspective Islam looks at people individually rather than the whole of society. This means economic polices will look to cater for all rather then just leaving satisfaction to the market. This is achieved by a host of rules Islam has in ensuring wealth distribution and government involvement in the economy that ensures the economy moves in the direction Islam has designated for it.

Islamic Macroeconomy

The Islamic economy follows a philosophy which is very different to Capitalism, as a result the end objectives of both economies attempt to achieve, widely differ and thus it would be invalid to measure one against the other as they both have different foundations and aims. Islam has detailed laws on the distribution of wealth and this is its ultimate aim with the economy – to ensure wealth circulates around the economy so all can share in the wealth that is generated.

The Islamic Macroeconomy in essence is a collection of rules which cater for society as a whole by removing all obstacles to the distribution of wealth. This is achieved by the Islamic economy not having a twin economy with a financial sector that operates in parallel to the real economy. The Islamic economic system does not recognise the financial markets in their current form and has made the Public Limited Company (joint stock (share)) companies haraam for a number of reasons. Fundamentally this type of contract contradicts the Islamic rules for contracts. The company in the West represents a particular type of contract - the 'Solitary Will,' this is where an individual agrees to the written constitution of a company by purchasing its shares with no formal offer from anyone. This has come to be termed as the Individual Will whereby shares could be exchanged very quickly without the need for two people to continuously sit down and have a formal offer and acceptance. An example of this was the take-over bid for the world's richest football club, Manchester United FC by Malcolm Glazier in 2005. He imposed his will on the company (i.e. he brought shares) and even though other shareholders were against such an action it was a legal form of acquiring ownership even though there was only one person in the contract. Most contracts involve two parties where one party offers terms and the other accepts, however under corporate law in the West setting up a business is a contract of 'solitary will.' It is not a contract between two or more people; rather it is an agreement that stipulates that all parties agree to it when they subscribe for shares in the company. So an individual joins himself to the conditions of a company – through purchasing their shares. This means to become a partner one does not need approval from the existing owners – this contradicts Islam.

With the replacement of such company structures with the Islamic company structure the speculative damage caused by shareholding will be removed. Shares are equally divided transferable notes which represent the value of a company at a particular time in question and not at the time of establishment. Purchasing shares makes one part owner of a company, as one has a share in it. Thus shares, stocks and equities are names for the same thing; they represent a transferable paper comprising of all the value of the company. The development of finance over the last 100 years has resulted in shares becoming no different to a currency. Money is defined as any item that acts as a "means of exchange," this is why shares, bonds, currency, treasury bills etc are all viewed as money as they are accepted as modes of exchange. Their values rise and fall depending on the worth speculators place upon them, it is for this reason share prices are monitored daily and they change every minute. The split between the company and shares is so wide that shares rise and fall completely independent to the company they are meant to represent. Shares are transferred between speculators as currency and this result's in the wide fluctuations on the financial markets which cause financial crisis and recessions. This type of ownership is not permitted by Islam hence the problems caused by their existence would not exist.

In Islam the rules for company structures are derived from the ruling for partnerships. This is because companies are an extension of a partnership. In origin this is a contract between two people over terms; in corporate law in the West they see giving charity, claiming insurance and the launching of a company and trade as the same type of contract whereas in Islam these are different types of contracts. This effectively means the absence of such types of companies will end the speculation they bring and will ensure speculative bubbles will never develop, bringing stability to the overall economy.

The Khilafah has been designated by Islamic evidences to play a direct role in the economy; Islam has also ordered the Khilafah to directly intervene in the economy in any cases of an imbalance outside its normal area of intervention. Islam made the Khilafah state responsible for the management of public property. Public property is the permission of the lawgiver to the community to share the use of an asset. Assets which are public property are those which the Lawgiver stated that belong to the community as a whole, and those which individuals are prevented from possessing individually. Islam prevents individuals from owning public property because the overall responsibility is for the Khilafah and no citizen is entitled to assume this responsibility unless it was designated to them. Islam has designated any utility regarded as indispensable for the community, such that its absence would require people to search far and wide for it, as a public property. This means such utilities would be publicly owned and the revenue generated would be administered for the benefit of all citizens. This is built upon the hadith of the Prophet (SAW) narrated by Ibn 'Abbas:

"Muslims are partners in three things: in water, pastures and fire." (Abu Dawud) and,

"Three things are not prevented from (the people); the water, the pastures and the fire" Ibn Majah narrated from Abu Hurairah, and

"Abyadh ibn Hammal came to the Prophet (SAW) and asked him to grant him a salt laden land and he granted it to him. And when he left, one person in attendance with the Prophet (SAW) said, "Do you know what you granted him? You granted him the uncountable water (Al-'udd)". He (SAW) then took it away from him."

These evidences show that people are partners and associates in water, pastures and fire, and that individuals are prohibited from possessing them.

However, there were occasions where the Prophet (saw) allowed such public property to be owned by individuals. It is known that the Prophet (SAW) allowed water in *At-Taif* and *Khaybar* to be owned by individuals, and it was used for irrigating their plants and farms. Had the sharing of water been just because it is water and not because of the consideration of the community's need for it, then he would not have allowed individuals to take ownership of it. So from his permission to individuals to possess the water, it can be deduced that the *Illah* (reason) of partnership in the water, pastures and fire, is their being of the community utilities that are indispensable to the community. Hence anything that qualifies as being indispensable to the community is a community utility, which is considered a public property, whether or not it was water, pastures or fire i.e. whether it was specifically mentioned in the *Hadith* or not. Hence although the hadith mentioned just three things, the presence of a *shari' illah* (divine reason) allows its application to be extended through the use of qiyas (analogy) to cover all instances of 'indispensable community utilities'. Thus water sources, the forests, large pastures for livestock and the like are all public utilities as well as oil fields, electricity plants, motorways and coalmines. This would also include roads, rivers, seas, lakes, public canals, gulfs, straits and dams

This would also include all the uncountable and un-depleted (i.e. large deposits) of minerals whether they on the surface of the earth such as salt, coal, sapphire, ruby, and the like. As well as gold, silver, iron, copper, lead and the like. This includes whether they are solid like crystal, or fluid like oil. All of these are minerals, which are included within the meaning of the *Hadith*.

Islam ordained the Khilafah to play a very specific role in the economy and forbade individuals from owning utilities that are indispensable for society. In this way the state plays a direct role in ensuring essential utilities are developed and made available to the public. With the privatisation of utilities during the 1980's in the West such key resources were snapped up by companies, who then possessed direct control over essential utilities. Society today is at the mercy of multinationals who decide how much water, gas, electricity and petrol is made available to the public. This problem very clearly will not exist in the Islamic economy and with the absence of a parallel financial economy; activity will only take place in the real economy.

Wealth Creation vs. Wealth Circulation

The Islamic economy aims to remove all restrictions to wealth circulation, for this Islam allowed individual ownership of items and services although it restricted the means that could be used to acquire ownership. It has permitted the individual to freely dispose of what he or she owns, and clearly outlined the different ways this could be achieved. A key characteristic of Capitalist economies is the wide income and wealth disparities between the rich and the poor; this is primarily due to the existence of policies which severely hinder economic activity.

Understanding the importance of wealth circulation is best understood by viewing every person and all companies' incomes originating from another person or company. Taxes levied by the state are regarded as income for the state and an expense to individuals. The monies spent on projects by government and salaries paid would be income for the individuals and an expense to the state. The money spent by employees on goods is an expense to them and income to companies. Hoarding money or leaving it in a bank account would in fact take it out of circulation. This would lead to a fall in spending, which would reduce production and result in the complete stagnation of the economy.

The Removal of Interest (Riba) Aids Wealth Circulation

Interest today has become enshrined as a global standard. Some Muslims unfortunately have tried to twist Islam by stating Islam only prohibited excessive interest thus allowing it in small amounts and some have claimed that as Interest *(Riba)* was gradually prohibited hence any attempt to ban interest should be gradual. Pakistan and Indonesia have on a number of occasions attempted to ban interest and moved to remove any interest in the economy however pragmatism gave way to the rule of Allah (SWT) and interest remains an integral part of their respective economies.

*Alla*h (SWT) says *"And Allah has permitted trade and forbidden (all) Interest"* [al Baqarah: 275].

The term *Riba* (interest) as found in the above verse and in other verses of the Qur'an and *Hadith* came in a general form. This would thus include every form of interest and this is because it is a generic name associated with the letters *alif* and *lam* (the) - meaning that all forms of usury are included whatever its type, whether it is a *Riba* that was well known at the time of the Messenger of Allah (saw) or a *Riba* that is not known and therefore a new issue. Therefore, there can be no place for making *Halal* any form of *Riba*, because the prohibition has come in a general form. The general term will remain general unless there is evidence that restricts or specifies the term i.e. another evidence would need to be sought. In this case there is no evidence to specify it, so *Riba* can only be considered in its general meaning.

For many it is difficult to envisage economic life outside the Capitalist framework. In Western economies every economic model is based on the rate of interest, from investment decisions, consumption decisions, savings decisions to financing loans and purchasing housing. The effect of this is that spending and investment are unnaturally skewed. For example, the average person who buys a house is then stuck in the mortgage trap paying back extortionate amounts of interest for 20-30 years. This coupled with loan payments for cars and other luxuries severely erode people's disposable income. However, even after the costs of taxation and the costs of interest payments, people are left with some disposable income. The problem is then one of investment; simply put people will not invest if the rate of return of a business venture measured against the risk of the venture is offset by the interest that can be gained from leaving the money in a bank account to accrue interest. Another problem is spending is taxed by Value Added Tax (VAT), which is a tax on spending.

Simply put if the risk of the rate of return on an investment is offset by the rate of interest then one would leave their wealth in a bank account rather then actually invest it. Hence the incentive would be to save the money rather then to use (invest) it. Although interest is money sitting in an account which banks use for their investment, this money is still not circulating in the real economy as banks invest all their money in the financial markets. This means that money is held for a promised rate of return rather than invested on the actual production of goods, or the building of a plant etc. Although a bank may invest some of its money in the production of goods i.e. when it lends money, this money is in effect circulating amongst a handful of individuals and companies, hence the money continues to be sucked out of the economy. In most of the Muslim world only those aligned with the regimes and the corrupt receive large loans from banks and this money remains circulating amongst such elites.

In other words, interest restricts investment and hence is an impediment to the distribution of wealth.

Islamic taxation aids wealth distribution

The burden of taxation plays an important role in the circulation of wealth as the spending patterns of society are to a great extent affected by the amount of taxation one is liable to pay. Taxation is considered a huge burden by all whom are liable, especially today where taxation is both direct and indirect. Taxation in the West is progressive with the rates rising as one earns more, society is liable to pay tax on their incomes rather then wealth and then also expected to pay indirect taxes such as road tax, VAT and local taxes. This means the total tax burden is well above 50% of incomes, which is a staggering amount. More then half of the incomes earned by workers goes to the taxman.

Taxation in the United States is a complex system which involves payments to at least four different levels of government with multiple methods of taxation. US taxation includes local government, possibly including one or more of municipal, township, district and county governments. It also includes regional entities such as school and utility, and transit districts as well as including state and federal government. The National Bureau of Economic Research has concluded that the combined federal, state, and local government average tax rate for most workers is around 40% of incomes. This does not include indirect taxation.

Taxation in Britain involves payments to local government and central government (HM Revenue & Customs). Local government is financed by grants from central government funds, business rates and council tax. Central government collects income tax, national insurance contributions, and value added tax, corporation tax and fuel duty. Currently the direct tax burden is 34% of incomes.

The Islamic economy on the other hand has no concept of Taxation on income thus there would be no income tax or national insurance contributions as well as indirect taxation such as VAT, road tax etc. Islam rather tax's wealth only, this is money held for one year above a certain threshold. The wealth, which meets these two conditions, would be liable to tax at a flat rate of 2.5%. This means there will actually be much more money in the hands of society and with the absence of interest this would further act as an impetuous to invest money which results in continuous circulation in the economy as holding it in an account without interest would be meaningless, and would over a period of a year incur tax.

Under the Islamic economy the burden of taxation is much lower; this will result in a larger chunk of people's income being available as disposable income. Therefore two or three people could easily enter into a business contract to supply some of the demand in the economy for consumer or manufactured goods thereby creating more employment in the economy. Although the amount of money collected under the Islamic economy in taxation may be lower then what is considered normal today in the world, the Khilafah's budget will not necessarily need to be large as with the Islamic rules of wealth distribution citizens will all benefit with the increase in national wealth. The majority of the industrial world's national government budgets are spent on social security, and this will be a small problem in the Khilafah as the rules for wealth distribution cause a multiplier effect which increase economic activity which will lead to the creation of new jobs and business opportunities.

What we see in the West is a whole host of policies which hinder wealth distribution; this is what leads society to continually borrow to fund its basic needs. On top of this the West suffers from a huge misdistribution of wealth as wealth distribution is left to the free market, where the rich and powerful take a larger share. A large part of Islamic economics is dedicated to ensuring wealth distribution. Islam recognises the differences in the ability and strength of people and does not leave things completely to the 'market.' Islam allows government intervention in the economy to bring equilibrium into the market. This is understood from the *ayah "That it (i.e. the nation's wealth) does not become a commodity between the rich among you."* (TMQ Al-Hashr: 7) This verse addresses the Khaleefah (leader of the Islamic State) to ensure that wealth is not distributed in a manner where it remains amongst the rich alone. Hence Islam allowed government intervention to bring equilibrium in the economy. Examples of these are when monopolies develop, restricting access to markets so prices rise or the discovery of a resource or mineral on land owned by an individual who restricts its distribution etc. In both cases and amongst others, the state would intervene keeping a balance between the basic needs of individuals and the misdistribution that has occurred.

Interest, the financial markets today, income related taxes and debt fuelled investments (speculation) all take wealth out of circulation. The more wealth changes hands the more economic activity proceeds. If wealth is removed from circulation exchange becomes scarce. Hoarding money or leaving it in a bank account would in fact take it out of circulation. This would lead to a fall in spending, which would reduce production and result in the complete halting of the economy. Hence the Islamic economy concentrates on wealth circulation rather then wealth creation, and with the absence of such obstacles, all citizens take part in the wealth generation process and then benefit from the results.

Islam's Monetary Policy

Inflation for decades has been considered a curse and modern plague; today it is seen as a necessary evil and part and parcel of 21st century life. Inflation is the general overall increase in prices across the economy, in most countries across the world over 2000 essential items are placed in a basket and their prices are compared to different time periods in order to asses prices movements.

The fundamental problem with rising Inflation is that it erodes the purchasing power one has. If prices were to rise and one's income remained the same then the amount one could purchase prior to the rise would be much lower after the price rise. Hence it is possible that an economy could be growing, but rising inflation actually means society is worse off. Inflation will always remain a problem in the West due to their ability to print money at will.

The ability to print currency at will creates a destabilising effect in the economy. Assets such as property and land have intrinsic values, but due to the effects of money creation the amount one can purchase with their money continues to fall. What we see in the West currently is due to the fact currency can be printed freely; governments regularly print more money, which is then chasing the same number of goods. The net effect of this is that although there is more money in the economy the purchasing power (ability of money to buy goods and services) falls and hence in real terms wealth is actually falling, because money is being devalued. Although the economies of the West post spectacular economic growth, in reality growth does not mean more, because price rises due to money creation cancels this out.

Thus the ability to print money at will is the cause of Inflation.

The Islamic economy has detailed rules on the legal tender which have the affect of containing inflation. Islam designated Gold as the primary monetary standard of currency and has allowed other metals to exist alongside Gold. It also made the issuing of currency the duty of the state, which doesn't allow banks to print currency.

This means the printing of currency is stripped from banks in Islam. Currently the world's banks practice fractional reserve banking whereby they lend more money then they actually have in deposits. This creates a big problem in the economy as very little equity can be used as collateral to borrow large sums of money; this is what creates a financial bubble. In the Islamic economy banks act in a similar fashion to venture capital firms collecting people's wealth and investing it around the economy, then distributing the profits amongst its depositors, alongside normal deposit functions. In an Islamic economy only the wealth the bank has in its possession can be lent thus removing the ability of banks to create money and transferring this to the central treasury - bait ul mal.

In Islam when it comes to exchanging a commodity with a specific monetary unit, Islam has guided us to the monetary unit by which the exchange is to take place. It has restricted the state to a specific type of money, which is primarily gold and silver. The Islamic evidences have designated gold and silver as the primary measuring unit for prices and labour. This is understood from the actions of Muhammad (SAW) when he collected zakat, levied taxes and imposed fines, all were measured according to gold and silver. Hence in the Islamic economy the currency would be pegged to both gold and silver. This would mean the notes and coins circulating in the economy would all be backed by gold and silver. This will no longer make possible the free printing of currency as the state would need to increase the actual holdings of gold and silver. This would end the problem of inflation as this has always been down to the ability of governments to freely print money. The curtailment of inflation in this manner will ensure the stability of prices across the economy and any increase in prices will be short lived and down to exceptional circumstances such as an earthquake damaging crop fields.

Islam put emphasis on wealth circulation and seeks to guard people's wealth by ensuring that its policies do not devalue money. The Islamic economy does not print money as it pleases since all its currency is backed by gold reserves. This means that the currency itself has a value relative to all assets. So this means that the value of land to a consumer will always remain in proportion to the value of gold. This creates stability in the value of the States currency. Furthermore, since the Khilafah does not print money freely, then there will not be an increasing amount of money chasing the same number of goods; hence the Islamic system is inoculated against inflation, since the main factor behind inflation is the easy printing of money.

This means that as businesses make more profits and acquire more wealth; their wealth is not devalued due to money creation, since it keeps its value. So in the Islamic system wealth increases and the Islamic system aids this, whereas the capitalist system increases money, but decreases wealth. The underlying cause of this is the fact that money in capitalist countries floats freely and is not linked with anything of intrinsic value; hence Western countries can print money, either by direct printing or by the money multiplier effect carried out by the banking system.

The Khilafah and Inflation

Islamic history clearly shows when the Islamic rule of currencies was followed the Islamic lands suffered little or no Inflation. The occasion's where inflation was problematic was when the Islamic rules were not adhered to.

The type of inflation experienced in early Islamic history was different in nature from the one experienced in 12th century under the Mamlukes. On most occasions the rise in prices was sharp but short lived. Instances of 'a sustained upward trend in the level of prices' were rare. There were instances of a gradual rise in prices at a low rate caused by continued influx of gold and silver. Also there were brief spurts of rising prices due the climatic conditions or disruption in transportation that caused a failure in supply leading to sharp rise in food prices.

The disintegration of the Abbasids resulted in the debasement of currency and the excessive issue of subsidiary (copper) coins (fulus) and the circulation of large quantities of counterfeit coins that caused spurts of inflation. These, were, generally, localised and temporary. Protests from the populace often resulted in cancellation of new issues and rectification of debasement. The large influx of gold and silver (new money) was absorbed by an expanding economy with widespread foreign trade. Egypt during the Mamluk period was specially afflicted by Inflation and when the situation did evoke a response from the authorities it was in the form of arranging additional supplies of food grains and by reducing import duties i.e. instead of increasing money supply as the West continually does today, the Khilafah increased supply. Another example of this was the early Ottomans, in 1507, 58 silver *aspers*, the Ottoman unit of currency, could buy one gold coin. 82 years later, in 1589, 1 gold coin cost 62 silver *aspers*, an inflation rate of only 7% over eight decades.[19]

Putting an end to debasement of currency and meeting price rises by arranging for increased supply are policies rooted in Islamic history. The two fiscal policies widely used in the world today of reducing public expenditure (with welfare provisions bearing most of the cut) and increased taxation (and domestic borrowing) are doubly doomed and not practical.

The Islamic Economy Promotes Entrepreneurship

Many critics of the Islamic economy argue that the Islamic economy offers very little incentive to invest as there is no interest *(Riba)* in the Islamic economy thus there will literally be no rate of return. Unfortunately many modernists from amongst the Muslims have been seduced by Capitalism and have continued to advocate such a view.

Islam promotes investment and relies on factors which promote real wealth. The Islamic taxation system does not tax income, but taxes wealth. This means that the average person will have more disposable income to spend on goods and services, and will be liable for tax on whatever wealth is left at the end of the year. The effect of this is that it will increase demand for goods and services right across the economy which will generate an increase in trade and in turn an increase in wealth for businesses. Since the investments that are open under the Islamic economy are not interest bearing, one will have no choice other than to invest in an Islamic business that is trading in goods and services. So ones wealth will be re-invested in businesses around the economy which will be used to invest in land or labour, creating more jobs within the economy. All of this will create a dynamic economy which creates more jobs. As more jobs are created, then more money is spent in the economy or re-invested in the economy, which creates more jobs in turn.

In essence with the absence of the parallel financial economy one can only invest in the real economy and this is achieved in primarily two ways:

1. With the absence of all policies which restrict wealth circulation, consumers will have much more to spend which will increase national consumption. The demand for items and services beyond the essential items means this will be a huge area for investment opportunities.

2. Although Islam designated ownership of public properties to the state, this means ownership of such items remains with the state, the state can make use of private companies to complete projects of whichever type along the supply chain of such utilities, this represents another investment opportunity for entrepreneurs. Ownership of key utilities will always remain with the state; the extraction, development, refining or construction can be undertaken by companies who will be paid for such a contract, this would be considered *Ijarah* (hiring or employment)

In the Islamic economy individuals can come together to fulfil any demand in the economy and for this Islam outlined very clearly the rule for company structures. Companies *(Sharikah)* are essentially a contract where people come together and the way they are compensated or paid is by distributing the profits amongst themselves. In origin a company is a contractual matter and Islam has laid down detailed rules for contracts. Islamic contracts must contain an offer and acceptance between partners over something i.e. over the thing they will trade in. Thus there are always two parties or more in the formation of a company. The work they do forms the subject matter of the contract because this is the reason they have come together. One of them as a minimum must be able to dispose on behalf of the company i.e. make purchases, dispose of assets etc, as a result Islamic companies came to be defined as the following:-

1. The Company of Equals *(Al-'Inan)* this is where both partners put their money into a business and work with it. Both partners or all the partners would have the right to buy and sell and take the company forward, hence they are all equal in their deposal.

2. The Companies of Bodies *(Al-Abdan)* this is where two or more people come together with their skills such as a consultant, doctor or craftsmen. So although they use their money, the skill they have is what constitutes the basis of the company.

3. The Company of Body and Capital *(Mudharaba)* this is where one funds the capital of the business and the other partner works with it. The partner who provides the capital element is a silent partner and takes no part in the running of the business. The other partner buys and sells on behalf of the company.

4. The Company of Reputation *(Wujooh)* this is a company similar to *madharabah* but the capital is provided by a silent partner who has respect and standing and based upon this the company trades. The partner could be a rich merchant, which would mean debts will always be paid by this company as they are backed by a rich merchant.

5. Company of Negotiation *(Mufawadha)* this is any combination of the above.

Whilst the consumption of goods is emphasised by Capitalism Islam emphasised spending and made it a virtue. Imam Nawawi narrated in his collection of hadith Qudsi that Allah said, "spend, oh son of Adam and I will spend on you". Islam recognised the need for spending to keep the economy dynamic. Furthermore Muhammad (saw) emphasised the giving of gifts from that which people like for themselves, and Islam even stipulated that this gift shouldn't be demanded back. The Prophet said "We do not set the bad example; the one who claims back his grant is like the dog which returns back its vomit". Islam even rewarded the one who gives a loan to his brother, and elevated the status of the loan to represent the reward of sadaqa, if he loaned his brother money twice. The prophet (saw) said; "No Muslim would give another Muslim a loan twice, except that one would be written for him as charity."

This means the Islamic economy will take a shape and form very different to what we see in Capitalist nations. Because the Capitalist belief idolises consumption, this has created a society steeped in greed and individualism, where the few care little for society and are even prepared to make money from the misery of others. The result of such values has led to many Western governments setting up regulatory bodies and passing legislation as a counter effect. In affect governments are legislating against the problems created by the Capitalist belief. Islam on the other hand enshrined spending and the state does not need to enforce this, since it will exist within the mentality of Muslims living under an Islamic economy. As can be seen in the West the influence ones belief has on their actions, this means no policy can enforce a trait like this, unless it comes from the very belief.

All of this demonstrates that the Islamic system has checks and balances that ensure wealth is distributed around the economy and does not remain in the hands of a few wealthy people which we see in the free-market system. The Islamic economy represents a compelling model which ensures wealth distribution continually occurs unhindered creating a multiplier effect with multiple investment opportunities. As the Islamic economy is derived from the Islamic texts compliance to it is an act of worship which will ensure corruption, greed and individualism doesn't creep into the Muslim mindset.

Capitalism: A history of financial crisis

The Dot.Com Crash, 2000

During the late 1990s, stock markets became beguiled by the rise of internet companies such as Amazon and AOL, which seemed to be ushering in a new era for the economy. Their shares soared when they listed on stock markets across the world, despite that fact that few of the firms actually made a profit. The boom peaked when internet service provider AOL bought traditional media company Time Warner for nearly $200 billion in January 2000.

The dot.com boom in reality was a bubble waiting to burst and in March 2000, the bubble burst, and the technology-weighted NASDAQ index fell by 78% by October 2002. The crash had wider repercussions, with business investment falling and the US economy slowing in the following year, a process exacerbated by the 9/11 attacks, which led to the temporary closure of the financial markets.

Long-Term Capital Management, 1998

The collapse of hedge fund Long-Term Capital Market (LTCM) occurred during the final stage of the world financial crisis that began in Asia in 1997 and spread to Russia and Brazil in 1998. LTCM was a hedge fund set up by Nobel Prize winners Myron Scholes and Robert Merton to trade bonds. The professors believed that in the long run, the interest rates on different government bonds would converge, and the hedge fund traded on the small differences in the rates. But when Russia defaulted on its government bonds in August 1998, investors fled from other government paper to the safe haven of US Treasury bonds, and interest rate differences between bonds increased sharply. LTCM, which had borrowed a lot of money from other companies, stood to lose billions of dollars - and in order to liquidate its positions it would have to sell Treasury bonds, plunging the US credit markets into turmoil and forcing up interest rates.

The US Federal Reserve decided that a rescue was needed. It called together the leading US banks, many of whom had invested in LTCM, and persuaded them to put in $3.65 billion to save the firm from imminent collapse.

The Crash of 1987

US stock markets suffered their largest one-day fall yet since the great depression on the 19th October 1987, when the Dow Jones Industrial Average index of shares in leading US companies dropped 22% and European and Japanese markets followed suit. The losses were triggered by the widespread belief that insider trading and company takeovers on borrowed money were dominating the markets, while the US economy was entering into an economic slowdown. There were also worries about the value of the US dollar, which had been declining on international markets. These fears grew when Germany raised a key interest rate, boosting the value of its currency. Newly-introduced computerised trading systems exacerbated the stock market declines, as sell orders were executed automatically. Concerns that major banks might go bust led the Federal Reserve and other major central banks to lower interest rates sharply. "Circuit-breakers" were also introduced to limit program trading and allow the authorities to suspend all trades for short periods.

The crash also showed that global stock markets were now closely linked, and changes in economic policy in one country could affect markets around the world.

US Savings and Loan Scandal, 1985

US Savings and Loans institutions were local banks which made home loans and took deposits from retail investors, similar to building societies in the UK. Under financial deregulation in the 1980s, they were allowed to engage in more complex, and often unwise, financial transactions, competing with the big commercial banks. By 1985, many of these institutions were all but bankrupt, and a run began on S&L institutions in Ohio and Maryland. The US government insured many of the individual deposits in the S&Ls, and therefore had a big financial liability when they collapsed. It set up the Resolution Trust Company to take over and sell any S&L assets that it could, including repossessed homes, taking over the bankrupt institutions.

The cost of the bail-out eventually totalled about $150bn.

The Crash of 1929

The Wall Street crash of 1929, "Black Thursday," was an event that sent the US and the global economy into a tailspin, contributing to the Great Depression of the 1930s. After a huge speculative rise in the late 1920s, based partly on the rise of new industries such as radio broadcasting and car making, shares fell by 13% on Thursday, 24 October. Despite efforts by the stock market authorities to stabilise the market, stocks fell by another 11% the following Tuesday, 29 October. By the time the market had reached bottom in 1932, 90% had been wiped off the value of shares. It took 25 years before the Dow Jones industrial average recovered to its 1929 level.

The effect on the real economy was severe, as widespread share ownership meant that the losses were felt by many middle-class consumers. They cut their purchases of big consumer goods such as cars and homes, while businesses postponed investment and closed factories. By 1932, the US economy had declined by half, and 33% of the US workforce was unemployed. The whole US financial system also went into meltdown, with a shutdown of the entire banking system in March 1933 by the time the new President, Franklin Roosevelt took office and launched the New Deal.

Many economists on both left and right have criticised the response of the authorities as inadequate. The US central bank actually raised interest rates to protect the value of the dollar and preserve the gold standard, while the US government raised tariffs and ran a budget surplus. New Deal measures alleviated some of the worst problems of the Depression, but the US economy did not fully recover until World War II, when massive military spending eliminated unemployment and boosted growth.

Overend and Guerney, 1866; Barings, 1890

The failure of a key London bank in 1866 led to a key change in the role of central banks in managing financial crises. Overend and Guerney was a discount bank which provided money for commercial and retail banks in London, the world's financial centre. When it declared bankruptcy in May 1866, many smaller banks were unable to get funds and went under, even though they were otherwise solvent. As a result, reformers like Walter Bagehot advocated a new role for the Bank of England as the "lender of last resort" to provide liquidity (cash) to the financial system during crises, in order to prevent a failure of one bank spilling over and affect all the others (systemic failure). The new doctrine was implemented in the Barings Crisis in 1890, when losses by a leading UK bank, Barings, made on its investments in Argentina, were covered by the Bank of England to prevent a systemic collapse of UK banking.

Secret negotiations by the Bank and London financiers led to the creation of an £18 million rescue fund in November 1890, before the extent of Barings' losses became publicly known.

South Sea Bubble 1720

The South sea company was an English company granted a monopoly to trade with South America under a treaty with Spain. In return for its exclusive trading rights the government and the company convinced the holders of around £10 million of short-term government debt to exchange it with a new issue of stock in the company, who's main activity was adventuring into the unknown Americas and coming back with riches.

In 1719 the company proposed a scheme where it took over nearly half of Britons national debt replacing it with company stock and hoping the steady repayments would be a source of income. The company then set to talking up its stock with 'the most extravagant rumors' of the value of its potential trade in the New World which was followed by a wave of 'speculating frenzy. This method, while winning over the heads of government, the King's mistress, etc., also had the advantage of binding their interests to the interests of the Company: in order to secure their own profits, they had to help drive up the stock. Meanwhile, by publicising the names of their elite stockholders, the company managed to clothe itself in an aura of legitimacy, which attracted and kept other buyers.

When the riches did not arrive on British shores in the numbers speculators had been lead to belief the south sea bubble burst. Its success caused a country-wide frenzy as citizens of all stripes – from peasants to lords – developed a feverish interest in investing; in South Seas primarily, but in stocks generally. The bubble reached over £1000 per share by August 1720 and collapsed to £150 by September. Speculation drove the price of the company's shares to inflated levels and when its promises never materialised speculators left on mass.

Conclusions

Most analysis on the credit crunch and the subsequent Food and Oil crisis have delved into technical detail on the financial markets and the motivation of the different players. There are a number of related wider issues which are missed and by understanding these Capitalism only remains due to the leg up it is receiving. These issues are:-

1. Speculation has left the global economy more vulnerable to a financial collapse than at any time since the Great Depression. The supposedly sophisticated models used by finance houses, a stock-market crash such as the one in 1929 was likely once in 10,000 years. They said the same, however, about the stock market crash of 1987, the collapse of the hedge fund Long Term Capital Management in 1998 and the sub-prime crisis. The obvious conclusion is that these models are flawed.

2. There is plenty of evidence that, in Britain, the US and elsewhere, those in government see little wrong with the system as it is. Democratically elected governments have, over the past three decades, willingly ceded control of the world economy to a new elite of freebooting super-rich free-market operatives and their colleagues in national and international institutions like the IMF, the World Bank and the World Trade Organisation. These 21st century Capitalists, who earn that title by their remoteness from everyday life and their lack of accountability, have gained this control on a prospectus every bit as false as much of the promotional material for their services. Their record is dismal:

- They promised economic stability - and have delivered chaos and volatility.
- They promised an economic order based on enterprise and personal effort - and have delivered one based on chronic indebtedness and wild speculation.
- They promised a "transparent" future in which all costs and prices would be clearly laid out and have delivered a world of bizarre and complex financial knowledge.
- They promised greatly increased wealth for all and have unleashed havoc on both the poor and professionals.

But none of this should be surprising. The 21st century Capitalists are hostile to - job security (other than their own), social tranquility and the traditional aspiration for both the good life and the quiet life. They roll their eyes when they hear that the factory worker, the Argentinean shopkeeper or the 50 year old women in Sialkot is complaining that their way of life is under threat. Meanwhile, elected politicians bend over backwards to make life as pleasant as possible for them.

3. Growth in the West has relied excessively on speculation in two forms: that in the financial markets and by home-owners. Economically, the legacy is a debt-driven, lopsided and unequal in which the pay of those at the top rises at 10 times the rate of those at the bottom. Instead of taking on the financial markets, Western governments have turned its attentions to the workforce - which has to be made ready for the global challenge from China and India by being re-skilled and re-educated and by learning how to be 'entrepreneurial'. Furthermore, the majority is routinely subjected to ever more illiberal, intrusive and obnoxious interference from state agencies, whether in terms of visual surveillance and the proposed identity card scheme, or in terms of being instructed to change their 'attitudes' on a range of subjects.

4. On the eve of the industrial revolution the world was sold the idea that the free market would be remarkably good at providing both peace of mind and material advancement. Living standards would rise for all; financial crises would be rare, banking crises rarer still. However 150 years later the free market has offered neither faster growth in living standards (for at least 99% of the world population) nor peace of mind. The modern era has been characterised by slower growth in average real incomes, higher levels of debt to maintain living standards, greater job insecurity and financial crises that have become more frequent and more far-reaching. The only class that has benefited unambiguously from the new world order has been the free markets extremists, just as the only creed that has been accepted has been their creed.

5. The sector of the economy which created the current mess is also the one that has benefited most in the last few decades. International banks had always tended to have global reach, they could benefit more than any other sector from more rapid communication, it was in their interests to have barriers on capital removed, they picked up hefty fees for organising privatisations, and competition allowed them to wipe out weaker competition. What was not really apparent until 2007 was how powerful the finance sector has become in the West. In countries like Britain, the expansion of the City of London had been the engine of the economy's growth - the fastest-growing parts of the finance sector expanded at around 7% a year between 1996 and 2006. Meanwhile, manufacturing output stagnated. Developing the finance sector as argued by its proponents, was good for a country like Britain. It allowed the country to specialise in what it was good at; it made London the hub of global finance, encouraged innovation and - by allowing the market to decide where capital

should go - made the economy more stable. However economic growth did not accelerate, productivity did not surge, there was no miracle cure to the balance of payments and only rare glimpses of the trickle-down effect.

6. Privatisation in developing countries was heralded as a way of preventing corrupt ruling cliques from siphoning off profits into Swiss bank accounts. Globalisation was specialisation on a grand scale: the logical conclusion to the sort of division of labour that Adam Smith and David Ricardo had envisaged 200 years ago. The modern world not only means that we can keep in touch by email with the world and buy an agreeable automobile from a Mexican factory, but also allows our pension fund to buy shares in an Indian software company. On paper, this life of greater choice, freedom and opportunity sounded splendid. In reality, however, the world doesn't work this way - and that's because what Capitalism has in reality created is speculation, recklessness, greed, arrogance and over-indulgence.

7. The activities of the big banks and the hedge funds in the first half of 2007 had no noble purpose: far from making prudent investments with societies pensions, they exploited the poor - the granting of mortgages to those who couldn't really re-pay them. The large financial sector has created a lopsided economy, Instead of having a broadly based productive economy supporting a financial sector that had investment (speculation) as one of its lucrative but less important activities; a diminished productive sector supported an ever-bigger financial sector that saw speculation as the very reason for its existence.

8. Greed has now come to infest all those in search for riches, and always has been, a factor motivating those who buy and sell shares,

bonds, currencies and commodities. What we have witnessed is the money lust becomes so pronounced that it crosses the dividing line between stupidity and criminality. Since 2002, a wave of mis-selling has been evident in the US real estate market, with tales of pensioners with only a tiny amount outstanding on their loans tricked into re-mortgaging their homes at ruinous rates of interest by unscrupulous mortgage brokers.

9. Those responsible for the speculative bubble of 2007 could not conceive that one day it would burst. That was where their arrogance kicked in. Their activities were making massive profits, a good chunk of which were being paid out in seven-figure bonuses that kept property markets humming. Even when cracks started to appear, they blamed everyone but themselves.

10. Bob Diamond, the chief executive of Barclays Bank in London, earned £22m in 2006 and was the sort of person who saw no reason why his money-making activities should be curtailed by red tape. But in August and September 2007, once the going had got tough, Diamond conducted a vigorous campaign against the Bank of England's Mervyn King for failing to provide the same sort of help to banks in the UK as was being provided by the Fed or the European Central Bank, which had stepped in after its banks were on the verge of collapse. As one commentator noted, this state of affairs was tantamount to the police being forced to provide a getaway car to bank robber's for fear that even greater damage would be caused by not doing so.

11. The response to the market meltdown illustrates some fundamental problems that govern the modern world. Despite the lip-service paid to democracy, western societies are in effect run by Capitalist money oligarch's, who have as little time for their wage

slaves as did Victorian England. In February 2008, two weeks after the British governments U-turn on the taxation of non-doms, the Labour government opposed a private member's bill designed to give greater rights in the workplace to agency workers - part-time workers who face some of the lowest wages and toughest working conditions in the West.

12. This crisis has proven very clearly that the apparent strength of the financial markets was illusionary. The happy-go-lucky mood evaporated instantly, with the write-down of losses accompanied by the sackings of executives and followed by more stringent lending for the real victims of the credit crunch. It is a principal of Capitalism that there is never too much of anything: never too much growth, never too much speculation, never too high a salary, never too many flights, never too many cars, never too much trade and never too much Oil. It was for this reason that the financial crisis was accompanied by rising inflation - as demand for oil and food pushed up prices globally.

13. This crisis has stunned both the left and the right of the political spectrum and the different economic schools of thought. Many economists and policy makers have ranted about more regulation and transparency with only a few highlighting the role greed and speculation played. As the crisis gets worse and continues to engulf the wider global economy Western governments continue to be unable to convince the populace with any long term policies which will deal with the crisis.

14. In the midst of such an unprecedented crisis Islamic finance is witnessing phenomenal growth with the global value of Islamic finance approaching $1 trillion. This has lead to some research and interest into Islamic principals however it must be borne in mind

that rather then viewing Islamic economics as a viable alternative global institutions see Islamic finance more as another money making opportunity. It is important to understand that Islamic finance in no way is the beginning of Islam being accepted; rather it is Capitalism making use of aspects of Islam it views as palatable where money can be made.

15. The current crisis represents an unprecedented opportunity to present the Islamic economic system, its details as well as the policies Islam has for some of the current problems. It should be explained to non-Muslims that Islam is much more then the prohibition of Interest *(riba)* and alms *(Zakat)* but rather a comprehensive system which makes the fulfillment of societies basic necessities (food, clothing and shelter) the aim of the system rather then economic growth. Islam makes people and their needs rather then production the central question which requires policies.

16. In presenting Islam and Islamic economic policy all the rules from the *Shari'ah* supplement each other and feed into each other, this means Islam is more then capable of being applied and in fact has a successful history of dealing with economic problems. When Islam reached India it destroyed the prevalent caste system, which allowed wealth to be distributed amongst the poor. It was Islam that introduced the concept of agency to the West which eventually became part of common law. Agency *(Hawala)* is where one can represent others in business and financial transactions, this stimulated trade and was the beginnings of what became the multinational company.

17. In presenting Islam it should be remembered Western society is drowning in the failure of Capitalism to tackle not just the financial crisis but a whole host of societal problems, in the US there is one

murder every 22 minutes, one rape every 5 minutes, one robbery every 49 seconds, and one burglary every 10 seconds, the financial crisis is just the tip of the iceberg.

Glossary

Bank 'run'	A type of financial crisis where panic leads to a large number of customers of a bank withdraw their deposits because they fear it is, or might become, insolvent. Because banks retain only a fraction of their deposits as cash the remainder is invested in securities and loans. No bank has enough reserves on hand to cope with more than the fraction of deposits being taken out at once. As a result, the bank faces bankruptcy, and will 'call in' the loans it has offered.
Collateral	A security or guarantee (usually an asset) pledged for the repayment of a loan if one cannot repay debt
Credit crunch	A credit crunch is a sudden reduction in the availability of loans (or credit) or a sudden increase in the cost of obtaining a loan from banks.
Credit rating	A credit rating assesses the credit worthiness of an individual, corporation, or even a country. Credit ratings are calculated from financial history and current assets and liabilities. Typically, a credit rating undertaken by a *credit rating agency* tells a lender or investor the probability of the subject being able to pay back a loan.
Deregulation	A term which gained widespread currency in the period 1970-2000, it is where governments remove, reduce, or simplify rules in the sectors that make up the economy. The stated rationale for 'deregulation' is that fewer and simpler regulations will lead to a

	raised level of competitiveness, therefore higher productivity, more efficiency and lower prices overall.
Default	This occurs when a debtor has not met its legal obligations according to the debt contract, e.g. it has not made a scheduled payment, or has violated a loan condition of the debt contract.
Derivatives	Financial instruments whose value changes in response to the changes in underlying variables. The main types of derivatives are futures, forwards, options, and swaps. In essence it is the betting of the movement in price of an underlying asset or security
Disposable income	This is gross income minus taxes and normal expenses (such as rent or mortgage, food, car payments, and insurance). It is the amount of an individual's income available for spending after the essentials (such as food, clothing, and shelter) have been taken care of. Disposable income is generally used as a measure of affluence and happiness in a nation.
Dividend	Payments made by a company to its shareholders. When a company earns a profit, that money can be put to two uses: it can either be re-invested in the business, or it can be paid to the shareholders as a **dividend**. Many companies retain a portion of their earnings and pay the remainder as a dividend.
Federal reserve	Central bank of the united states
Financial markets	A financial market is a mechanism that allows people to easily buy and sell (trade) financial securities (such as stocks and bonds), commodities

	such as precious metals or agricultural goods.
Fractional reserve banking	A banking practice in which banks keep only a fraction of their deposits in reserve with the choice of lending out the remainder while maintaining the obligation to redeem all deposits upon demand. This practice is prevalent worldwide and is considered to be the customary form of banking system
Government intervention	Actions taken by government within the economy to deal with market failure or imbalances which generally are left to markets.
Great depression	A dramatic worldwide economic slump that began in the US in 1928, and then spread to the rest of the world.
Hedge fund	A private investment fund that charges a performance fee and is typically open to only a limited range of qualified investors. Hedge fund activity in the financial markets has grown substantially and constitutes 30% of all US fixed-income security transactions, 55% of activity in derivatives with investment-grade ratings, 55% of the trading volume for emerging-market bonds, as well as 30% of equity trades. Total industry assets reached $2.68 trillion in 2007
Inflation	A sustained increase in the general level of prices, which is equivalent to a decline in the value or purchasing power of money. If the supply of money and credit increases too rapidly over many months, the result will be inflation.
Legal tender	A currency payment that, by law, cannot be refused in settlement of a debt.

Liquidity	An asset's ability to be easily converted through an act of buying or selling without causing a significant movement in the price and with minimum loss of value. A liquid asset is considered one that can be sold rapidly, with minimal loss of value and anytime within market hours.
Macroeconomics	A branch of economics that deals with the performance of the economy as a whole. Along with microeconomics, macroeconomics is one of the two most general fields in economics. Macroeconomists study indicators such as GDP, unemployment and price in order to understand how the whole economy functions.
Moral hazard	The prospect that a party insulated from risk may behave differently from the way it would behave if it were fully exposed to the risk.
NASDAQ	The National Association of Securities Dealers Automated Quotation System is an American stock exchange with the largest electronic screen-based equity securities trading market in the United States. With approximately 3,200 companies, it lists more companies and has more trades per day than any other US market
Nationalisation	The act of taking an industry or assets into the public ownership of a national government.
Re-mortgaging	Or Re-financing is the process of paying off one mortgage with the proceeds from a new mortgage using the same property as security.
Recession	The opposite of economic growth – where the economy shrinks. A country is considered in recession when it shrinks for two consecutive

	quarters.
Risk	The probability that an investment's actual return will be different than expected. This includes the possibility of losing some or all of the original investment. It is usually measured by calculating the standard deviation of the historical returns or average returns of a specific investment.
Securitisation	A finance process where assets, receivables or financial instruments are acquired, classified into pools, and offered as collateral for further borrowing. Due to securitisation, risky loans can be packaged with less risky loans in affect making the whole instrument investment grade.
Short Selling	The practice of selling securities the seller does not own, in the hope of repurchasing them later at a lower price. This is done in an attempt to profit from an expected decline in price of a security, such as a share or a bond. In contrast ordinarily one would 'go long' purchasing a security in the hope the price will rise.
Speculative attack	Actions undertaken by speculators involving the massive selling of a currency. This has much in common with cornering the market, as it involves building up a large directional position in the hope of exiting at a better price. As such, a speculative attack relies entirely on the market reacting to the attack by continuing the move that has been engineered, in order for profits to be made by the attackers
Solvency	A financial condition experienced by a person or business entity when their assets exceed their

	liabilities. A company is considered insolvent if its liabilities exceed its assets because it can no longer meet its debt obligations when they come due.
Stock market	A market where shares in companies are bought and sold
Treasury bonds	A debt security, in which the authorised issuer owes the holders a debt and is obliged to repay the principal and interest (the coupon) at a later date, termed maturity. Treasury bonds are US government bonds issued by the United States Department of the Treasury through the Bureau of the Public Debt. T-Bonds, or the long bond have the longest maturity, from ten years to thirty years.
Tiger economies	The 'tiger' economy was a term coined to describe South Korea, Singapore, Hong Kong, and Taiwan who underwent rapid growth and industrialisation in the 1960's and 1970's. The four Tigers share a range of characteristics with other Asian economies, such as China and Japan, and pioneered what has come to be seen as a particularly "Asian" approach to economic development, that of an export driven economy.
Venture capital	A type of private equity capital typically provided by professional, outside investors to new start up's. Typically money is made from the new start up profits rather then share price rises.

Bibliography

1 Naween A. Mangi, April 2003, *'And the worlds Top Market is….Pakistan,'* Business Week, retrieved November 2007

http://www.businessweek.com/bwdaily/dnflash/apr2003/nf20030410_4232_db039.htm

[2] Containing System Risks and Restoring Financial Soundness, Global financial stability report, IMF, April 2008, accessed 24th May 2008, http://www.imf.org/external/pubs/ft/gfsr/2008/01/pdf/text.pdf

[3] L Wroughton & J Topsfield, *'World's new crisis: soaring food prices,'* April 2008, accessed 27th May 2008, http://www.theage.com.au/articles/2008/04/14/1208025091644.html

[4] Federal Reserve Statistical release 2006

[5] i.e. those with a credit score (FICO) less than 620

[6] David Gow, Oct 3, *'If you try to control everything it would probably kill capitalism,'* Guardian, http://business.guardian.co.uk/story/0,,2182836,00.html

[7] Engdahl W, (2004) 'A century of war: Anglo-American oil politics and the new world order,' revised edition, Pluto press

[8] W Engdahl, *'Speculators knock OPEC of oil-price perch,'* Asia Times online, May 6th 2008, accessed 28th May 2008, http://www.atimes.com/atimes/Global_Economy/JE06Dj08.html

[9] Bank of England statistical release, M0 December 2007

[10] Tom Bowden, 'Citigroup writes off another $15.2 billion and plans 9,000 job cuts,' Times Online, April 2008, accessed 9th May 2009,

http://business.timesonline.co.uk/tol/business/industry_sectors/banking
_and_finance/article3775320.ece

[11] Bank for international settlements, Monetary and Economic
Department, Triennial Central Bank, *Survey of Foreign Exchange and
Derivatives Market Activity in April 2007'* Preliminary global results,
September 2007, Switzerland,
http://www.bis.org/publ/rpfx07.pdf?noframes=1

[12] Chairman Cox Letter To Basel Committee In Support Of New
Guidance On Liquidity Management, March 2008, retrieved 18th April
2008, http://www.sec.gov/news/press/2008/2008-48_letter.pdf

[13] BBC documentary titled "Spend Spend Spend," shown May 3, 2003,

[14] Chronic Hunger and Obesity Epidemic; Eroding Global Progress,
World Watch Institute, March 4, 2000

[15] Paul Krugman, MIT Professor of Economics, Princeton University,
How Washington Worsened Asia's Crash; The
  Confidence Game,
http://thenewrepublic.com/archive/1098/100598/krugman100598.html
and
  http://web.mit.edu/krugman/www/myth.html

[16] Yilmaz Akyüz and Korkut Boratav, 'The Making of the Turkish
Fonancial Crisis,' reterived 5th June 2008,
http://www.econturk.org/Turkisheconomy/boratav.pdf

[17] 2005 Economic, Survey, income data, US Census Bureau

[18] Carvel J, *'Super-rich have doubled their money under Labour,'* The Guardian,
December 8th 2004, Site Accessed 3rd

Nov 2006,
http://society.guardian.co.uk/socialexclusion/story/0,11499,1368919,00.html and HMRC distribution of
personal wealth', site accessed 3rd Nov 2006,
http://www.hmrc.gov.uk/stats/personal_wealth/13_1_delay_mar06.pdf

[19] Derived from original figures taken from research paper, Berument H and Günay A, (2004), Inflation Dynamics And
Its Sources In The Ottoman Empire: 1586-1913, Discussion Paper 2004/3, http://www.tek.org.tr Turkish Economic
Association